The Life and Writings
of
GIAMBATTISTA VICO

The Life and Writings

of

GIAMBATTISTA VICO

by

H. P. ADAMS, M.A.(CANTAB.)
*Lecturer in History at the University
of Birmingham*

NEW YORK / RUSSELL & RUSSELL

REPRINTED FROM A COPY IN THE COLLECTIONS OF
THE BROOKLYN PUBLIC LIBRARY

FIRST PUBLISHED IN 1935 BY
GEORGE ALLEN & UNWIN LTD.
REISSUED, 1970, BY RUSSELL & RUSSELL
A DIVISION OF ATHENEUM PUBLISHERS, INC.
BY ARRANGEMENT WITH
GEORGE ALLEN & UNWIN LTD., LONDON
L. C. CATALOG CARD NO: 72-102463
PRINTED IN THE UNITED STATES OF AMERICA

To

MY PARENTS

and

MY WIFE

PREFACE

A BOOK on Vico in the English language has long been overdue. The excellent short monograph by Flint, though no student of the subject should neglect it, was written before the publication of those works which, in our own century, have been devoted by some of the leading minds of contemporary Italy to their great countryman. It is hardly suspected by ordinary, educated readers in this country that, in a period of Italian history which they are accustomed unduly to despise, lived one of the most powerful thinkers and writers of modern Europe, a man about whose life and work there will grow up a literature such as has grown up around the supreme names in modern thought and culture. As such he is at length being treated in Italy. The *Bibliografia Vichiana* issued by Signor Croce is a great volume with several supplements.

Readers of the following pages who wish to make a further study of Vico should undoubtedly begin by reading his autobiography and the *Scienza Nuova* in its first form. They could then read Croce, *La filosofia di Giambattista Vico*, and Gentile, *Studi vichiani*, along with Vico's own earlier writings;—the inaugural orations, and the two short philosophical works, *de nostri temporis studiorum ratione* and *de antiquissima italorum sapientia*. Biographical interest may then be indulged by the reading of *La Giovinezza di Giambattista Vico* (1688–1700) by F. Nicolini, whose greatest contribution, however, to the study of Vico is the magnificent edition of the *Scienza Nuova* of 1744, showing all the variant readings of every edition of the *Scienza Nuova* after the first. This great and final form of Vico's thought should then be studied. Of the books which help us to understand the intellectual atmosphere of Vico's time, one of the shortest, and also the most interesting and enthusiastic, is by R. Cotugno: *La sorte di Giovan Battista Vico*. Among the writings by men who were Vico's contemporaries or nearly so, which help very considerably to understand that age, are the three very interesting autobiographies of Francesco d'Andrea, Spinelli and Giannone. Biography had a considerable vogue in Italy early in the eighteenth century; the eminent Arcadians all had their lives written and several of these are of interest to the student of Vico. A standard work on the history of the Italian intellect is that of Maugain: *Étude sur l'Evolution Intellectuelle de l'Italie de 1657 à 1750*. There is also an interesting work, *Les Cartésiens de l'Italie*, by Berthé de Besaucèle, who gives useful summaries of the writings of the leaders in the anti-scholastic movement of the time. Another part of the background may be filled in by reading Amabile's great and rich volume on the Inquisition.

Of books and essays which discuss different aspects of Vico's thought there are many. Those by Croce include *Ciò che è vivo e ciò che è morto della filosofia di Hegel, Le fonte della gnoseologia vichiana*, and two essays on Vico as a historian in *Nuove curiosità storiche*. Much of Signor Croce's work on Vico appeared in *La Critica*, including reviews of books and, above all, the continuation of the *Bibliografia Vichiana*. The aesthetic and philological theories of Vico have been studied very elaborately from a special but most illuminating point of view by A. Sorrentino in *La retorica e la poetica di G. B. Vico*. The editors of the *Rivista internazionale di filosofia del diritto* published important studies on Vico as jurist, *per il secondo centenario della "Scienza Nuova" di G. B. Vico* in 1925. Important essays on Vico's biography have been published by B. Donati as *Autografi e documenti vichiani inediti o dispersi.*

There is some very good work on Vico in German. Werner's book, *G. B. Vico als Philosoph und gelehrter Forscher* was published in 1881, three years before Flint. It is comprehensive and accurate, but devoid of the life brought into the subject of late years by the Italians. Otto Klemm's work, *G. B. Vico als Geschichts-philosoph und Völkerpsycholog* is a very useful study in the light of the teaching of Wilhelm Wundt. Two studies by Richard Peters, *Der Aufbau der Weltgeschichte bei Giambattista Vico* and *Aurelius Augustinus und Giambattista Vico*, excite an impatience to read the yet unpublished work of the same writer. A good example of the way in which Vico's thought is still a living influence is afforded by the *Kriegsvorlesung* (1916) on *Geschichtsphilosophie*, one of the latest utterances of Windelband. In French, after Michelet, I can only remember on Vico himself, besides the work of Besaucèle already mentioned, an interesting chapter in Monod, *La Vie et la Pensée de Jules Michelet* and some useful paragraphs by the Italian Professor A. Rava, in his *communication faite à la Sorbonne* (26.2.1927) on *Descartes, Spinoza et la Pensée Italienne*. In English, besides Flint, there are Vaughan's lecture on *Giambattista Vico, an Eighteenth-century Pioneer*, and a chapter each in J. G. Robertson's *Genesis of Romantic Theory* and Vaughan's *Studies in the History of Political Philosophy*, all three eloquent and suggestive. The principal works of Croce can also be read in English, including *La filosofia di Giambattista Vico* and *ciò che è vivo*, etc., which last has been changed in title to *The Philosophy of Hegel*.

My authorities on the thought of Ficino and Patrizzi are G. Saitta: *La Filosofia di Marsilio Ficino* and P. Donazzuolo in *Atti e Memorie della Società Istriana* (1912).

I wish here to acknowledge my gratitude to the Research Grants Committee of the University of Birmingham for their grants to meet the expenses first of typing my manuscript and finally of publishing this book.

The dedication is an inadequate recognition of sacrifices and encouragement.

CONTENTS

THE LIFE AND WRITINGS OF GIAMBATTISTA VICO

CHAPTER I

THE BOY

In the middle of the seventeenth century, when England was preparing the future of parliamentary liberty, when Holland was building up a wide Empire in the far East, and approaching the culmination of her greatness in the art of Rembrandt and the philosophy of Spinoza, and when France under Louis XIV was preparing to dominate the continent, the most ancient kingdom of Naples had been ruled for generations by viceroys of the kings of Spain. Thrusting out her promontories into the corsair-haunted horizons of the Mediterranean and threatened throughout her scattered mountain-hamlets with the depredations of native brigands, she had long ago seen the glorious republics on her western harbours dwindle to fishing-villages. The city of Naples itself, with memories going back to the ancient, Virgilian Sibyl, was now an overgrown capital where the architecture and the laws of imperial Rome lingered amid every form of parasitic life engendered by the decay of the middle ages, but where a new life of the mind was struggling into existence.

Ignorant of the world of thought into which he was penetrating, a country lad of fourteen tramping from his distant village found work, about 1650, in the heart of it all, the *Strada de' Librai* or Neapolitan Booksellers'

Row. Although never able, to the end of his days, to write other than a clumsy childish hand, he came to have his own shop there and to be the father of the greatest Italian thinker of the age. He had common sense and cheerfulness, but apparently very little ability. His second wife, the mother of eight children of whom Giambattista, born in June 1668, was the last but two, was an affectionate, rather sad woman unable to sign her name. The heredity of Vico's intellect cannot be traced; that of his temperament may be faintly manifest.

We know his childhood only as it was mirrored in the autobiography which he wrote at the age of fifty-seven. But he seems to have belonged, like Rousseau, Alfieri and Byron, to that order of men of genius who remember vividly the emotions of the earliest recollected years. At the age of seven, he had already begun to go to school, "a spirited boy, impatient of rest," when a fall on a staircase fractured his skull. A tumor grew in the wound and a series of exhausting operations was considered necessary. The surgeon predicted that he would either die soon or become an idiot. So vivid an early experience was perhaps enough to make recollection intense. He attributes to it in part his tendency to melancholy, which was also his maternal inheritance. But he adds, characteristically, that this disposition was not unconnected with the nature of his intellect. Readers of *Tristram Shandy* will remember that Tristram's tutor was to be both acute and argute. The terms have since gone out of fashion; acute minds were deeply penetrating, whilst arguteness was a more superficial cleverness and plausibility. We should perhaps translate "argute" by "ingenious"; but "ingenious," or *ingegnoso*, had with Vico a different sense, it was rather inventiveness or the power to discover new truth. It was a power belonging to minds that are acute, and Vico thinks his early melancholy marked him as one of this order of men.

For three years he was unable to go to school. He gives us no account of this interval. For months he must have been unable to read and the home was miserably narrow; there was only one room over the little bookshop. Such houses were common enough, and the very cooking was often done outside with a portable stove. The building opposite was an establishment for assisting the poor with loans, a semi-eleemosynary pawnshop. Down the long street were booksellers far busier and more opulent than his father. There was the enterprising Frenchman Bulifon "at the sign of the Siren," who edited a gazette, wrote guide books and sent his sons to finish their education like young nobles with a grand tour of Europe. There was Bulifon's enemy, the Neapolitan Parrino, author of a popular history of Naples, and editor of a rival gazette. In and about such shops the boy saw the principal writers, lawyers and ecclesiastics of a city in which those professions were more than commonly overcrowded. In the streets he would be familiar with the sight of monks and beggars. Bishop Burnet, who visited Italy a few years later, has much to say of these monks. "The convents," he writes, "have a peculiar privilege in this town; for they may buy all the houses that lie on either side till the first street that discontinueth the houses; and there being scarce a street in Naples where there is not a convent, by this means they may come to buy the whole town. . . . The preachings of the monks in Naples are terrible things. I saw a Jesuit go in a sort of procession with a great company about him, and calling upon all that he saw to follow him, to a place where a mountebank was selling his medicines; near whom he took his room and entertained the people with a sort of farce, till the mountebank got him to give over, fearing lest his action should grow tedious and disperse the company that was brought together."

Vico's home was in the heart of old Naples, near to the historic churches and monasteries, to that of St. Gregory the Armenian, his father's landlord, and to the great building dedicated to St. Laurence, where the ancient parliaments of the feudal kingdom had formerly been accustomed to meet. A few streets away was that far from quiet place the university. The noisiest and most animated scenes would be the sunny markets of the fishermen and fruit-sellers, a source of anxiety and profit for the Genoese tax-gatherers to whom the kings of Spain had pawned the revenues. The child must also have stood in a vast crowd awaiting in breathless awe the city's annual miracle, the liquefaction of St. Januarius' blood. But he wandered farther afield, for in later years, when he wished to illustrate the magnifying imagination of children, he remembered how the hills outside the city had to his young eyes been mountains and precipices.

In 1678, at the age of ten, he was well enough to go to school. The system of teaching then in vogue was still that of the middle ages, with modifications introduced chiefly by the Jesuits in the preceding century. The medium of all higher education was the Latin language. The Latin grammar was therefore the principal if not the only subject taught to a small boy in his first two or three years. The third or lowest department of the school, the grammar school, was set apart for it, and consisted of two or three classes. The work of the class in which Vico was placed was found too easy, but he was not ready for the class above. He obtained, however, permission to cover the intervening ground by private study, and "astonished the master with the spectacle of a boy conducting his own education."

Soon afterwards his father was persuaded to remove him, to place him in the hands of the Jesuits themselves, the dominant educationists of the age. He now found himself no longer in the grammar school. He was received into the second or middle school, that of the humanities. Here the chief task was the reading of the Latin classics. Mediaeval teachers had never taught these for their own sake, but for the sake of enabling the young cleric to use and to understand the language of the church, the young lawyer that of the law. The Renascence on the other hand treated the study of ancient culture as an end in itself. The Jesuits, anxious to meet the man of the world on his own ground in every sphere and to bind all the arts to the chariot of religion, trained their pupils to compose readily and with clearness in the language that was still the vehicle of controversy and to some extent of affairs, a language whose masters yet afforded the growing modern literatures an unsurpassed lesson in the logic of style. From the Renascence they adopted likewise a greater respect for the individuality of the pupil, seeking to excite emulation rather than fear. In Vico, emulation was easily excited to excess. Pupils were pitted one against another as in the disputations of the middle ages, only here it was more often a competition in the recitation of Latin poems. Combats would sometimes last for weeks;

whole teams might be engaged. Vico writes at fifty-seven as if the emotion of juvenile gladiation vibrated in him still. His antagonists were the three most formidable that could be found. The first was vanquished; the second became ill through the effort; the third was promoted to a higher class to save him from defeat, like a hero in the Iliad caught up in a cloud by his protective deity. This injustice, and the fact that, through not being himself promoted, he would have to repeat in the second semester the work of the first, provoked him to absent himself from school until he had finished unaided the whole course of the humanities.

The highest school was that of logic or philosophy and he entered it in October 1681. On this topmost level the student emerged at length to behold the end and purpose of his grammatical and memorizing toil. That culmination was nothing but the old scholasticism, the mediaevalized Aristotle, whose greatest interpreter was Aquinas, or, at the most modern, the Jesuit Suarez. Into these schools the liberating thought of Galileo and of Descartes had not penetrated. The speech of the middle ages echoed on every side. Of Vico's two teachers one was a nominalist, the other a realist. Vico had the worst possible fortune at the start. The particular scholastic logicians recommended to him by the nominalist Balzo were two of the most useless and perplexing—Petrus Hispanus and Paulus Venetus. Modern authorities are emphatic on the uselessness, dryness and difficulty of these and their like. Prantl, who wrote the history of them, expresses the hope that his own work will make it unnecessary for anyone after himself to read them. Renan says no life or thought circulates any longer under the

hard rind of their terminology, which has been rarefied
and complicated until no sense or truth remains within.
The young Vico was altogether confounded. He gave up
study for eighteen months. So little idea had he been
given of anything interesting in this world, in geography,
in astronomy or in history, that for one who could not
hack his way through the jungle of scholasticism nothing
seemed left but the idleness of despair. This defeat was
perhaps his first important victory. In knowing that he
did not understand Petrus Hispanus and Paulus Venetus,
he probably had the advantage of some of his teachers.
What he wrote at the beginning of his autobiography was
true; he had a probing mind; he was not to be hypnotized
by words. His intelligence had revolted, perhaps also his
nervous system. He was only fourteen and his application
was intense. He says that often his mother, waking
from her first sleep and seeing him still reading at the
table, would tell him for pity's sake to go to bed; frequently he studied all night.

After a fallow period of eighteen months, an event
occurred which again placed intellectual pursuits before
him in an attractive light. This was "on the occasion of
the restoration after many years of the *Infuriati*, a famous
academy, in San Lorenzo, where were gathered together
the principal advocates, senators and nobles of the city;
he was spurred on by his genius to resume the abandoned
way, and started forth once more. This most beautiful
fruit is rendered to our cities by the illustrious academies:
youths, whose age by reason of good blood and little
experience is full of confidence and lofty hopes, are
incited to study for the sake of praise and glory."

His teacher when, in the summer of 1683, he returned

to the Jesuit college, was Giuseppe Ricci, a scholastic certainly, but of a more attractive sect than Balzo's. He was a Scotist. In the "abstract substances" with which his pupil now became acquainted there seemed "more reality" than in the "modes" of the nominalist. In the pleasure with which Vico deserted subtle elaborations of terminology and formal logic for the promise of something conceivable hovering in the region beyond appearance, he found afterwards a "presage" that he would be drawn to Plato. Moreover, he says that Ricci, though Scotist in sect, was fundamentally Zenonist, and the Zenonists were in contact with the science of the time. Taking their name from Zeno of Elea, they theorized on the mathematical qualities of space and time. But Vico became impatient as day after day was spent in endless descant on the theme of "ens" and "substantia." Hearing that Suarez had reasoned about everything that could be known, not only as a metaphysician should but in a style that was clear and easy to read, he retired from school yet again and spent a year upon Father Suarez. This reading brought his knowledge of scholasticism up to date. Suarez was a Jesuit of the preceding century and still their great authority. The young Descartes, in a Jesuit college in Paris, had been brought up on him. There was an element of Zenonism in Suarez; there were thoughts approaching the speculations of Galileo on the nature of space and matter. But what Vico says he learned in Suarez was the Aristotelian philosophy. And this, he found, gave him no help as a basis for his later studies.[1] He does not ostentatiously turn his back on scholasticism, as did Bacon, for example, or Giannone. He none the less leaves it behind. With his ambition to read the greatest and hardest work on each subject he studied, he might easily have been one of those who fall victims to their predecessors in the field of learning, thinking over again the complicated systems of thought which, like an endless maze, stretch themselves out in front of ambitious youth. But, with an instinct for what was alive, he leapt over the wall.

CHAPTER II

LAW AND POETRY

FOR a poor, but clever and studious youth, it was natural that his father chose law as a profession. A successful advocate could make a great fortune, and there were innumerable consolation prizes for mediocrity. Giambattista was sent to an expert crammer, Francesco Verde, who, like many others, systematically broke the law against university teachers having private pupils. Influential connections prevailed against attempts at control; but once he was placed under arrest for three days, and thereafter for some time paraded the streets daily with a bodyguard of two hundred students. When Vico went to him in 1684 he had become a canon of the cathedral and was at the height of his reputation for successful coaching. The legal system of Naples was a jumble of all the codes that had superimposed themselves each on its predecessor during the political and dynastic revolutions of all the centuries from that of Justinian. In such a chaos judicial decisions were highly arbitrary. Notes taken in the lecture room of an efficient coach were most important for examinations and were even quoted in the courts. Antonio Vico was naturally astonished when his son, after about two months, decided to go to these classes no more, saying he could learn nothing there. The memorizing of notes, even the notes of important cases, was poor food for the intellect. Giambattista struck into his old line of studying in private the works of the greatest writers. A certain kindly doctor of laws named Giannattasio, not much known in the courts but very learned and a great collector of books, had procured through the elder Vico a copy of *Vulteius on the Civil Institutes*. The compliant father consented to ask for the loan of it. Giannattasio wanted to see the young man, and was so pleased with his reasons for leaving Verde that he gave him the book and with it *Canisius on the Canon Law*.

For an intending practitioner some experience of the courts was much to be desired. About the end of 1685 or the beginning of 1686, in his eighteenth year, Vico was placed under the guidance of the advocate del Vecchio, described by him as a very honest man who died poor. A few months later it happened that Antonio Vico was prosecuted by a fellow bookseller. The argument of the defence was entrusted to Giambattista with assistance from del Vecchio and proved successful, winning praise from the opposing counsel. But the atmosphere of the courts repelled the young philosopher who felt "an ardent desire for leisure in which to pursue his studies."

He was now in the habit of writing verse—"in the corrupt style of the age," that is to say Marinism, Gongorism, metaphysical poetry or by whatever name the literature of the baroque age may have passed in different countries. Looking back, he calls his attempts at this period exercises of *argutezza*, cleverness, and a necessary relief from the dryness of law and metaphysics if a young mind over-strained by rigid processes of thought was not to lose all spontaneity. An old and kindly Jesuit father had acquired fame in Naples for sermons in the same taste—Giacomo Lubrano. To him the young versifier one day took a canzone on the subject of the rose, modestly asking him to correct it. The old man was pleased with it and read him an idyll of his own on the same subject.

We can see for ourselves the sort of "conceits" with which the old preacher and the young student entertained themselves, for some poems of the former have recently been republished, ingenious sonnets about sleep, about some fantastically cut cedar-trees, about magnifying-glasses which are "the hyperboles of the eyes," about iced drinks, about Phyllis, in whose bosom a silkworm had hatched itself out, so that her fair breasts were the sunrise of life to a humble worm; the preacher could moralize on Death without recourse to the graveyard, since, here too, dead dust had quickened into wormy life. This poetry was compounded of many ingredients, of the exaggerated fancifulness into which the freedom of the Renascence flowered when it was over-ripe, the Euphuism of self-conscious aristocracy and courtliness of style, the attempt of a philosophical and scientific age to express in verse the results of speculation and experiment. There was realization that novelty was the soul of art, but no clear vision of what the new age had to do in poetry. There was dissipation, therefore, and exploration in verse of a mental world growing less and less poetical.

CHAPTER III

VATOLLA[2]

ABOUT eighty miles south of Naples the bay of Sorrentino is guarded by an extensive mountainous promontory, the Monte Stella. Here, about three miles inland, with a view of the historic islands of Capri and Ischia, are the village and the castle of Vatolla, amid cultivated slopes and groves of chestnut, oak and olive. In 1686 there were about two hundred and fifty inhabitants. Men and women alike laboured in the fields, the women occupying their spare time with spindle or distaff. The village had its own tailor and shoemaker, but no physician.

The eminence which closed the view towards the East and the Apennines was crowned by an old monastery of the Carmelites. Nearer to the village, on a lower hill, is the parish church of Santa Maria delle Grazie, so much altered now as to have been almost rebuilt, but possessing still the humble baptismal font, the altar and the one or two religious pictures once familiar to the eyes of Vico. Below the village are a chapel and monastery of still greater interest. The chapel, built at the end of the sixteenth century, commemorated the miraculous cure of a lame beggar in the act of saving a picture of the Virgin from the flames. Within the neighbouring Franciscan monastery, piled up in a couple of cells, Signor Nicolini, reverently exploring, came upon some three hundred volumes, somewhat extensively despoiled by many generations of mice. They are the library of which Vico had the use for about nine years. Over against the building is a row of olive-trees, and here, according to local tradition, Vico used to sit and meditate.

To explain how he came to escape from the city into this lofty retreat we must again turn to the autobiography. He was eighteen years old, had been studying law for more than a year and had just won a lawsuit for his father without being drawn by this initial success into any affection for the proposed career. Consumed with intellectual hunger, feeble in body for he was threatened with consumption, entirely without money and shrinking from becoming an advocate, a notary, a monk or a small bookseller, he stood in need of a special providence, and this he received. Geronimo Rocca, bishop of Ischia and brother of the lord of Vatolla, was at this time living in Naples, occupied with the printing of one of his books. Vico had as yet only touched the fringe of intellectual society. But in one of the bookshops he met the bishop and conversed with him about the best method of teaching jurisprudence. "Monsignor was so well satisfied with his views that he wanted to engage him to teach his nephews in a castle of the Cilento, a place beautifully situated in a most pure air. It belonged to his brother, Signor Domenico Rocca, whom Vico"—the autobiography is written in the third person—"came to know henceforth as his most kindly Maecenas, and as one who took pleasure in the same kind of poetry. Vico was assured that he would be treated in every way just as Domenico's own sons were treated, and so it proved in fact. He was promised health from the good air, and all the leisure he needed for study."

If we had nothing but the autobiography to guide us we should suppose that Vico now lived at Vatolla for nine years beginning in 1686. It is probable, though not certain, that we should be right, both as to the date of his arrival and the time when he came back to live permanently at Naples. But it is certain that he was not at Vatolla continuously all those nine years. The Roccas had a house in Naples and another at Portici. Every year they spent some time in Naples, and there are documentary traces of Vico's presence there with them. Looking back, he may well have thought of these years as having been passed altogether away from the scenes of his earlier and later struggles and privations. They are the years in a man's life when what is read—especially if his chief occupation is with books—takes from the emotions of early manhood a tinge of lasting poetry. For Vico it was the poets, orators and historians of ancient Rome and mediaeval Italy and the philosophers of the Renascence who became associated for ever with sunsets over the gulf of Palermo and noontide in the oaken shades around Vatolla, and with that seat under the olives before the old monastery with its legendary memories.

He gives no account of his pupils. The eldest of the four was fourteen, the youngest, Zaverio, the only one worth naming, since he was later involved in a political conspiracy of which Vico was the historian, was only nine, a thoughtful boy with chestnut hair. That his relations with them were happy, that he owed much to the family, that he neglected no duty or service on their behalf are facts which all the evidence appears to substantiate. It is equally true that during these nine years he planned and completed a magnificent course of reading and self-education.

The autobiography was designed as a history of mental

development. It was written nearly forty years later than the date at which we have now arrived; that is to say, at a time when the writer's system of thought was, in its main outline, complete. The journey was described after the destination had been reached. For the years in which Vico was producing, we can control the autobiography by means of his other writings, and we shall find that in some degree his attainment coloured his retrospect. For these earlier years we must accept his assurance that what was important to him afterwards occurred to his mind at the time when he says it did. There is no reason to doubt that, when in his last year at school he passed from a nominalist to a realist master, he had a foretaste of the satisfaction he afterwards found in Platonism; nor that, when he sought a philosophical basis for jurisprudence, the Aristotelian system he had "learned in Suarez" proved inadequate. He attributes to the period of his first legal studies the attempt to systematize his thoughts on jurisprudence. At least, what he says is that he found supreme pleasure in a particular double approach to the subject. He liked, in the first place, to reflect on general principles, secondly, to observe the detailed interpretation of the ancient texts. The general principles he found in the old interpreters, who had applied abstract ideas of justice to the various motives of equity which had determined emperors and jurists in judging particular cases. But he says that only later did he come to see that these interpreters were philosophers of natural equity. Similarly, in mentioning the pleasure he had in the diligence with which jurisconsults examined the letter of decrees and edicts, he says that afterwards he regarded these jurisconsults as the historians of Roman civil law. This way of putting it has verisimilitude. It is our own fault if we antedate the relation in Vico's mind between philosophy and history.

Coming to the time of his legal studies at Vatolla he strikes again the same two notes, and with fuller meaning; for he now made a direct application of moral philosophy to jurisprudence. Horace's *Art of Poetry* taught him that the richest source of poetical suggestion was to be found in moral philosophers. His mind was very much on poetry at this time, perhaps with Lubrano's compliments fresh in his recollection, perhaps also to amuse Domenico Rocca. So he commenced reading Aristotle, the more so as his legal writers often referred to that philosopher. Returning to jurisprudence, he claims that he now saw more clearly the significance of its double aspect. The jurisconsults had evolved an art of equity; it consisted in innumerable precepts extracted by them from the reasons of the laws and the will of the legislators. The science of the nature of justice, on the other hand, which was the concern of the moral philosophers, proceeded from a few eternal truths, and these were dictated by metaphysics, the metaphysics of ideal justice. With a side thought on the inadequacy of current modes of instruction in law, he plunged further into metaphysics. It was now that he found the philosophy of Aristotle inadequate to his problems. Apparently he read very little of Aristotle; he says he had learned him in Suarez. He turned to Plato, "guided only by his fame as the prince of divine philosophers."

The reasons he gives for preferring Plato to Aristotle show that he understood neither of them. He thought that Aristotle's metaphysic involved a conception of God as working on the universe from without as a potter moulds his clay. He attributed to Plato the belief in an eternal idea like a seminal spirit, educing and creating matter from itself; the ideal of justice was accordingly at the basis of things, and on it Plato constructs his state. The cause of Vico's confusion is very plain when he tells us that at this time he was reading some half-dozen Italian neoplatonic authors of the fifteenth and sixteenth centuries. From them he imbibed the notion of emanation as explaining the creative activity of God. This he confused with the conception of God as immanent, ascribing it to Plato himself.

He attributes the dawn of a new synthesis in his mind to this doctrine of a world ruled by divine ideas, a doctrine to which he says he was being led at the same time by the study of theology. He had brought from home a book on the doctrine of grace, written by the French Jesuit Etienne Deschamps in opposition to the Jansenist interpretation of Augustine. He says that Deschamps shows the position of Augustine to be midway between the extremes of Calvin and Pelagius. "This disposition," he explains, "enabled him [Vico] afterwards to meditate a principle of the natural right of the nations, which should be both apt for the explanation of Roman and all other civil law of the gentiles in respect of history, and should agree with the sound doctrine of grace in respect of moral philosophy." This passage is closely parallel to that in which he gives the result of applying his supposed Platonism to jurisprudence, from which, he says, there dawned on him "without his being aware of it, the thought of meditating an ideal, eternal law set forth in the idea or design of Providence in a universal state, upon which idea have since been founded all the commonwealths of all times and all nations"—certainly without his being aware of it, for the time when he becomes aware of it is much later; and when he adds that this ideal republic "should have been contemplated by Plato in virtue of his metaphysic, but could not be, since he was ignorant of the fall of the first man," Vico is enunciating his own theory of many years later.

Thus the reading of Aristotle in order to get suggestions for poetry led to unexpected paths, along which he made some progress at Vatolla, though he was far as yet from suspecting the heights to which they would bring him. Another important part of his self-education was somewhat similarly initiated. When he left Naples his idea of poetry was much the same as Lubrano's. In the Franciscan library at Vatolla, found in such evil case in our time by Signor Nicolini, he read a dissertation on the metres of Virgil. This revealed to him how mistaken a course he and his contemporaries were following. Reading Virgil, probably for the first time since he had been at school, he "was filled with such admiration that he conceived the desire to study the Latin poets, beginning with their prince." He studied not only the Latins and not only the poets. He read Latin and Italian authors on alternate days, comparing Cicero with Boccaccio, and Dante or Petrarch with Virgil or Horace. All these he read three times, first in order to understand the unity of composition, then to study the transitions and the way in which the theme was developed, finally for the passages which seemed to him remarkable in conception or expression. These last he noted on the books themselves, never copying them into a commonplace book, since they were only to be appreciated in their context. In each case he found the Latin writer superior in language to the Tuscan. This course of reading gave him that intimate knowledge of the mind of past ages without which all theorizing about history is a building without foundations. He commenced it when he was eighteen or nineteen and pursued it probably during a good part of the next eight or nine years, concurrently with jurisprudence and philosophy.

It has already been mentioned that his idea of ancient philosophy was only in part drawn from his very slight acquaintance with Plato and Aristotle at first hand. His philosophers were in reality modern authors, though they were authors whom modern readers were leaving behind. He names several of them, whose neglect in his own time he deplores. In Ficino, the light of early Medicean Florence and first interpreter of Plato to modern Europe, he found much that we can trace in his own work. For Ficino thought and action were one in the will of God; liberty and necessity likewise. By the act of creation God brings into being a universe permeated throughout with his own nature. Throughout the whole of this universe there is a perpetual tendency to return to its divine source. In this doctrine of man's participation in God's nature and creative activity Vico may well have seen something midway between Calvin and Pelagius. Ficino says, as Bruno and Vico say after him, that the soul is entire in every part of the body as God is entire in every part of the universe. This, too, is Augustinian. Thought creates its object, and, both in Ficino and in the earlier writings of Vico, geometry is given as the example. Ficino went beyond Vico.

This thing is God,
To be man with thy might,
To grow straight in the strength of thy spirit
and live out thy life as the light.

There was something of this in Ficino. It was this that the Reformation and Counter-Reformation suppressed.

Vico names second Ficino's greatest disciple, Pico della Mirandola, who had in common with his master the neoplatonic doctrine of emanation and the purpose of reconciling Platonism with Christianity. He carried the eirenic attempt much farther, assuming one esoteric doctrine to underlie all systems of thought from Moses to the end of the middle ages, even the systems that seemed most antagonistic to one another. But this was a secret which only the mystic under divine guidance could find out. In reading this writer Vico could feed his desire for a great historical synthesis and could fancy that he was entering into the thought of mankind at very early ages. He was fostering his tendency to exalt imagination and memory above exact and minute analysis and becoming familiar with a pantheism which influenced him in spite of his fear of it. The belief in a transmitted early wisdom was one which he had to shed before his own conception of history could shape itself.

We make a steep descent in passing to Agostino Nifo, the parasite of Leo X. But Vico was sorry to see the once popular Latin essayists of the Renascence going out of fashion. There was nothing profound for him to learn in the works of Nifo, though some passages appear to have yielded him suggestions. The opening words of a brief treatise comparing the merits of the soldier and the man of letters are almost identical with the first sentence of

Vico's fifth academic oration. Both writers emphasize the barbarity of war if not controlled by men of culture, and both insist on the usefulness of the arts and sciences to a military commander. But Nifo's argument is not Vico's and has no depth or originality. Both say that moral science is useful to a general, Nifo in a weak chapter of quotations and examples which contribute nothing but a reassertion of the statement, Vico in a comparison between municipal and international law, showing the responsibility of an independent commander in time of war as a judge between nations.

Matteo Acquaviva, Duke of Atri, was just the reverse of a professional writer like Nifo, with whom he was almost contemporary. He deals, in the intervals of an active life, with what interests and puzzles him. Commencing to write on moral virtue, he is quickly involved in the problem of the nature of mind. He writes on the mathematics of music and astronomy. He shows a wide acquaintance with ancient authors and quotes especially Pythagoras, Plato, Aristotle, Zeno the Stoic and Plutarch. These quotations were possibly the most important part of his works for Vico, in an age for which much ancient thought was filtered through such books.

Agostino Steuco, librarian at the Vatican under Paul III, in his work on the perennial philosophy, led Vico at much greater length through a history of esoteric thought whose stages illustrated more or less the thesis of Pico della Mirandola. Vico must have spent weeks over this curious history of philosophy in its very readable Latin. It is worth while to remember that he was at one time in the habit of reading at considerable length about the times between Adam and Abraham, treated as a basis for elaborate speculation. Steuco has a neoplatonic trinitarian doctrine, and is struck by the resemblance of the Mosaic "I am" with the Platonic conception of God as pure Being. Vico, too, is deeply impressed by this and may have had his attention drawn to it by Steuco, though it would be misleading to make much of their common emphasis on such a commonplace of Christian Platonism. Steuco is not much of a philosopher himself but, such as he is, belongs to the Renascence, like all the rest on Vico's list of authors. He is no belated mediaeval schoolman. He is as clear as Machiavelli or Vasari about the reverse suffered by culture in the fall of the Roman Empire. Like some other neoplatonists he not only rejects the philosophy of Aristotle but also has a poor opinion of his character.

Quite a different aspect of the Renascence is presented in Alessandro Piccolomini, the keynotes of whose life and work are moderation, elegance and utility, whose favourite poet was Horace, and who regarded Aristotle as the safest guide on Earth, though Plato might open the way into the world divine. His treatise on education was on lines that Vico at any time would have approved. He thought rhetoric, embracing the whole art of speaking and writing, should be commenced early. He gave priority in general to the subjects which exercise imagination and memory. He makes much of Aristotle and Cicero and the ancient historians. The civil and practical bias throughout the whole scheme are quite in agreement with what his young reader was afterwards to recommend. In a brief treatise on the certitude of mathematical sciences Piccolomini deals with a problem which became central for Vico. The theory that mathematics has of all sciences the greatest certainty, derived from Aristotle through Averröes, was held, he thinks, by the schoolmen on wrong grounds. The true reason for the superior clearness of mathematical entities is that they are all quantities, and quantity is *omnium sensatorum sensatissimum*, the most sensible of all the objects of sense. He seems to mean, taking his argument as a whole, that in mathematics alone we can be sure we have the data of the problems investigated. Vico was to go deeper. Why are we sure we have the data? Because we have made them ourselves.

Francesco Patrizzi is mentioned several times by Vico, once for a translation from Proclus and again for theories on poetry with which Vico does not agree. He was a zealous Platonist, holding, like Campanella and Vico himself, that Plato was more in accord with Christianity than was Aristotle. His patron, Clement VIII, heard him with interest, but the authority of Aristotle was too firmly established in scholasticism to be officially repudiated as Patrizzi desired. He interpreted Plato through the neoplatonists, a rule adopted even by so sober a thinker as Piccolomini. To give him great importance as an influence on Vico is impossible, but to explain Vico it is necessary to accumulate the suggestions he received from his reading and environment. Patrizzi's teaching that space is the intermediary between mind and body, between the infinite Creator and the finite creation, and his attempt to elucidate a philosophy of geometry from the nature of geometrical points, may be kept in mind as bearing upon problems which we shall find occupying the attention of Vico.

Mazzoni, the last on Vico's list, was at Urbino in the

time of Tasso. In his philosophical work he labours the old theme of the fundamental agreement of all philosophies. He was a vain and plausible sophist and man of affairs. He had, however, the great merit of appreciating Dante, of whom there were only three editions in the whole sixteenth century. He held the poet to be a mine of information on the arts of civilization, and made an elaborate comparison in this respect between Dante and Homer. He anticipated modern scholarship in holding that Dante wrote in Tuscan, and not in a language collected from all the dialects of Italy. Vico at one time held the latter view, though at some period after 1725 he changed it for the former.3 For him likewise the comparison of Dante with Homer in relation to the life they image is of great moment, but he does not ascribe any of his ideas to Mazzoni.

We have now seen what Vico read at Vatolla. The Latin and Italian classics whom he mentioned were carefully studied. He had also lived through a century and a quarter of the Italian Renascence in philosophy, taking from it his idea of what the ancients taught. We must remember the character of the student. He more than once expressed his disdain of exact scholarship. His mind, as we can judge of it after he became a prolific writer, was always in a perfervid state of synthetic activity. The thoughts of such a mind, like heavy billows on sand, perpetually efface and transform the patterns over which they move.

Perhaps we may apply to him the words which another great imaginative writer used of himself. "When some years ago," writes Schiller, "I read the history of the Dutch revolution in Watson's excellent description, I felt myself in a state of enthusiasm which political history seldom affords. On a more careful examination I found that what had caused my enthusiasm was not something transferred to my mind from the books, but had been much more a swift result of my imagination, which had given to the subject-matter the form in which it had exerted on me so potent a charm."

Philosophy and philology had not put an end to the writing of poetry. He never ceased, as long as he could write, to produce occasional verse. But it was in his youth and at Vatolla that he wrote the one poem which moves us. He lived at this time amid the conditions for poetical creation. The neoplatonic authors gave an imaginative tinge to his philosophy. He filled his mind with Virgil, with Dante and with Petrarch, and we have seen that Virgil had reformed his taste. The world's taste too was changing. The *Précieuses Ridicules* had already been adequately ridiculed in France; the Augustan age dawned in England somewhere between the *Annus Mirabilis* and the composition of *Absalom and Achitophel*; in Rome, Arcadia was founded before Vico's final return to Naples; in Naples itself di Capua and others were turning to earlier Tuscan models. Vico's conversion was not in the same direction. There are common elements, especially in the adoption of classical form and the purgation of eccentricities. But the world was coming to think in prose, and to see in poetry not its prophetic soul but its elegant expositor. Vico, on the other hand, was attracted, not, like his countrymen, to della Casa, but to the "mighty torrent" of Dante. He did not soon reach the problem of his later brooding, that of the poetic nature of all early language. When he finally attained to this deep conception of poetry it was as a philosopher and not as a poet.

At Vatolla he listened to the mighty torrent of Dante. He had leisure to think and to feel. Though his prospects in life were uncertain, his powers were not exhausted from day to day; the poignancy of his inner struggles was not deadened by labour and routine. The glamour of life in adolescence and the melancholy with which it is often haunted were intensified by this very uncertainty, which was due not merely to external circumstances but to enfeebled health. In 1692 he reached a condition of despair in which he feared that his body would no longer answer the fierce requirements of his intellect. In this mood, and passing, it would seem, many hours in communion with scenes of touching natural beauty, he put his soul into a poem for the first and last time.

The *Affetti di un Disperato* commences with an almost ecstatic expression of the desire for self-probing and self-torment. He is tired out, he says, with the griefs that afflict the soul and haunt the obscurity of memory. These griefs are many and partly hidden from himself. "I know you not," he says, "but indeed I feel you." He challenges these sorrows, "if ever they are courteous torturers," to band themselves together, to come out of their darkness. He desires, as long as he lives, to keep pain alive in his heart as that which gives him life and may release him from his life.

Then he takes a higher flight and surveys the world of strife verging on catastrophe, with fates of unexampled potency arrayed for the destruction of man. The iron age is drawing towards its latest and deadliest tract of years. No blest light any longer shines from heaven and no happy soul can enter upon earthly existence. But the passage ends with an arrogant egoism of misery. Even amid these calamities, there is no one who is not enviable compared with the writer of these strong and bitter lines.

Then he unfolds the essence of his own peculiar misery. Every spirit that enters the world of breathing life takes up gladly the burden of the body and finds in it the instrument of well-being. Vico is an exception. His body will not answer the needs of his mind. Body and mind are mutually tormenting in a life without fulfilment and without repose. So the fierce pleasure of self-torment remains, and lest its expression should bring a deadening alleviation he will stimulate it by the contemplation of its opposite. This he does in a few lines which paint with delicate strength the happiness of a virtuous, temperate spirit, that loves and is beloved with the affection which is its own sole and sufficient reward, and lives amid merited honour and tranquillity. Thus, he says, with a baroque image to close the paragraph, his sad heart, like a red jewel through which ice appears as flame and milk as blood, can extract anguish from the ideal of human felicity.

A few more lines of fierce lament, moving with rapid and growing emphasis, give him again the opening for touching and luminous contrast. If from the bright quarter of the heavens has descended on him too the longing to kindle in beechen or laurel shades the beautiful light that makes souls illustrious—and this was in some degree the gift of his spirit when it veiled itself in the body's shadow—it has become now a penalty and not a benefit, since it gives him the clearness of vision which makes his suffering more intense. He blesses in contrast the rude pastoral existence of rustics, satisfied with their crude loves and sated with the fatigues of hunting.

He reaches the climax in a frantic appeal to heaven to rain still more miseries on him. If this be remitted, it will be only because the fates grudge him his melancholy pre-eminence among the wretched. He swears by the desolation of the forest that its utter silence shall be broken by no sigh from him. The afflicted heart desires desperately to feel nothing but its bitter suffering.

This poem was written in 1692, and the writer was twenty-four years old. As poetry, it is unique in Vico's work. The passages which rise to universality are beautiful and powerful. As autobiography the poem has importance as our only window into the writer's mind at a time for which no intimate correspondence has been preserved. The absolute character which he gives to his despair is baroque, but not Italian. The seventeenth century elsewhere was much occupied with the infinite, from Pascal shuddering at the void to Sir Thomas Browne who loved to lose himself in an *O! Altitudo!*4 It is perhaps a defect of Vico's poem that its central theme, on which the fine passages depend, is an affectation. But of a degree of unhappiness not incompatible with creative effort the poem certainly bears evidence, and perhaps of moods in which he feared complete frustration of his struggles. As the monument of a spiritual crisis it has great importance from the complete absence of religious motives either of consolation or of despair. There is no trace of religious self-examination. Iron fate rules the universe, and an evening twilight is descending upon the aspirations of man, upon those yearnings for temperate enjoyment or poetic fame in which the writer's spiritual satisfactions consist. No divinity inhabits either the stars from which the arrows of pestilence are directed on mankind or the lonely woods whose dead silence the stoical sufferer disdains to disturb with a sigh or a complaint. It is the first crisis in which he found an articulate voice. More than once in boyhood the growth of the soul had been checked, the stream had seemed to be dammed up. Now, in adolescence, the vacuity of prospectless existence was for the first time filled with a voice, the voice of his own genius.

CHAPTER IV

THE INFLUENCE OF CONTEMPORARIES

THOUGH so much of his reading would have been judged obsolete in the intellectual circles of the day, or perhaps for that very reason, Vico felt it essential to have access to the sources of living thought. He had long reverenced from a distance the men of established reputation in science and letters, and he envied those of his own generation who enjoyed their society. To have to rely on intermediaries, who might be unable or unwilling to transmit the vital seed, was a great misfortune. Before he finally left Vatolla, which he probably saw for the last time in 1695, he had ceased to be a stranger to the world of thinkers and writers in which he desired to have part.

The elderly leaders of intellectual life in Naples of that time were the heroes of an important revolution of culture. Naples had brilliantly illustrated the revival of letters towards the end of the fifteenth century, but before the middle of the sixteenth a Spanish viceroy had closed the academies, those gatherings of the real promoters of discovery and criticism, which were allowed to revive slowly from the second decade of the seventeenth century. About the middle of that century a remarkable group of men initiated a great intellectual advance.

A very few isolated individuals in the southern capital had kept in distant communication with the progress of the age of Galileo, of Bacon and of Descartes. It required a pilgrimage to find even the books of these thinkers, or of Hobbes or Gassendi. The throne of the mediaeval Aristotle was not yet cast down. He still governed the forum and the school. Before the turn of the century, however, certain students of natural philosophy, the academy of Colonna, were thinking on lines which may be described as atomistic, Gassendist or Galilean. They were interested in the physical basis of science. Their inspiration was rather Italian than foreign. To this academy succeeded that of the *Investiganti*, which included the chief instigators of reform. Three men were specially prominent, Francesco d'Andrea, Leonardo di Capua and Tommaso Cornelio. D'Andrea has left us an autobiography in which he describes his discovery, as a young man, that scholasticism was more fruitful of disputes than of invention. His profession of advocate was embraced early and his education specialized, but he found time later to interest himself in the scientific movement. He was admitted as a silent junior to the academy of Colonna. His fame as an advocate and publicist made him a tower of strength to the *Investiganti*. He has an important place in the history of Neapolitan jurisprudence. Through him the application of historical criticism to Roman law, dating from Alciatus and Cujacius, superseded in the courts of the city the mediaeval tradition of scholastic argument. He made the courts where he pleaded a centre of intellectual life. Men watched the cases in which he was engaged, not for the sake of seeing which side won, but in order to know what doctrines of jurisprudence had been enunciated. His studies in physical science were closely connected with his work as a jurist. They afforded the great example of inductive method. The physicists and mathematicians, the academy of the Cimento at Florence, a true lighthouse of experimental science to the whole of Italy, the successors of Galileo at Pisa, where Marchetti gave a stimulus to atomism by his translation of Lucretius, supplied the principles of investigation in other spheres of thought.

> The atoms of Democritus
> And Newton's particles of light
> Are sands upon the Red Sea shore
> Where Israel's tents do shine so bright.

These words of Blake might have been written of that exodus from scholasticism which took place in the seventeenth century.

The scientific manifesto of the Neapolitan group was the *Progymnasmata Physica* of Cornelio, published in 1663, containing several new discoveries which remind us that these were the early days of the Royal Society and of the first effective use of microscopes. It was Cornelio who had made the famous journey in 1649, from which he brought back the books of the modern philosophers to his thirsting friends. Vico may have witnessed the public funeral which d'Andrea secured for Cornelio in 1884, two years before the first sight of Vatolla.

Di Capua, the bosom friend of Cornelio, had influence in two directions. His profession was medicine. He brought the whole medical profession about his ears by his attack on their antiquated and unscientific methods, and with his theories of the rainbow he excited a controversy scarcely less resounding. But he was also at the head of a movement in letters. His industry was exemplary.

On a journey to Naples from the mountain village of his birth he once lost a thousand or so of his early poems in a capture by brigands. "Capuism" in literature was a reaction against the fantastic style of the preceding generation and an attempt to recover the qualities of earlier Tuscan writers. For this restoration of purity in Tuscan prose, Vico, in the autobiography, gives him qualified praise; qualified because he himself always aimed at importing into his Italian prose the subtlety of Greek and above all the majesty of Latin, and these qualities he missed in the limpid simplicity of di Capua. However, he mentions both him and the "very Latin Signor Cornelio" as prevailing influences at the time when he himself was beginning to write.

In those last years at Vatolla when Vico was certainly forming influential connections in Naples, Cornelio had been dead for some years; d'Andrea and di Capua were nearing the grave. Di Capua died in 1695 and d'Andrea in 1698. Their efforts had been crowned with a large measure of success both in the courts and the university, to the discomfiture of professors of the old school who, it was said, refused to look through a microscope lest they should see more than Aristotle had seen. Vico was commonly regarded as a disciple or partisan of di Capua, and however much or little he may have seen of the three great leaders he certainly entered society under the aegis of some of their best known associates, of men who were already bearing the brunt of controversy in the cause of progress.

This controversy was being waged in the two fields of philosophy and of politics. The same champions were engaged in both. The connection between the two lay in the power of the Inquisition, which lent the aid of its unconstitutional authority to the obscurantists in doctrine. The Inquisition was known to the kingdom of Naples in three forms. Against the ancient tribunal of the archbishop no legal objection was taken. The Spanish form had been successfully resisted in the sixteenth century. It was the Roman inquisition, exercised by papal delegates, which was now being challenged by the same group of writers and constitutional lawyers who promoted the study of modern philosophy and science.

Vico rightly distinguished two movements of free-thinking about this date—the atomist, Epicurean or Gassendist tendency at the time of his first departure for Vatolla, and the Cartesianism of which he became increasingly aware towards the time of his final return to the city. He mentions them slightingly as transient fashions, ignoring the fact that in atomistic physics men were laying the foundations of modern science and that Cartesian rationalism was an influence in whose current, whether he admitted it or not, he himself was for some years to live and move and have his being.

The fear of Descartes had first made the Inquisition uneasy about Naples in 1671, when Vico was three years old. "There is reason to suspect," wrote the Holy Office in Rome to the Archbishop of Naples, "that there are persons in the city who, to give proof of their mental superiority, promote the philosophical opinions of a certain Renée Descartes, who some years ago gave to print a new philosophical system reviving the ancient opinions of the Greeks concerning atoms, and that from this doctrine certain theologians pretend to demonstrate how

D

the accidents of bread and wine remain after consecration when the substance has been changed into body and blood." It is clear that the congregation had heard of the atomists and of the attacks made on Descartes with reference to the Eucharist, but scarcely knew what was in his books. A mind that only knows two facts puts them together.

When the archbishop, acting as delegate of the Roman inquisition, succeeded in obscuring the distinction between his different capacities, he was able to use unobtrusively the detested methods of the Roman tribunal, with all its secrecy, especially in regard to the names of witnesses. He could often, in spite of the law, ship off his prisoners to the dungeons at Rome. But more than once in recent years a separate Roman delegate had arrived to exercise the jurisdiction of the Holy Office ostentatiously. The catholic majesty at Madrid was not indifferent to his royal rights at Naples even as against the Holy Father. With the throne occupied by the sickly and childless Charles II the shadow of partition was beginning to influence policy. It was important to secure loyalty by conciliation. Burnet had observed a mitigation of Spanish haughtiness in social intercourse. Ostentation on the part of the Roman inquisitor led on two occasions to his expulsion. The struggle was in a critical stage during Vico's later years at Vatolla. The inquisitor imprisoned a number of people on suspicion of their being "atomists" and Epicureans. There was immediately a constitutional opposition. The days of Neapolitan parliaments had long since passed, but within the city a time-honoured right of meeting pertained to certain noble families and to representatives of the middle class. This organization in *sedilia* was very old though it cannot, as used to be thought, be traced to the phratries of the ancient Greek colony. Its opposition, led with great skill and moderation by eminent jurists, procured the expulsion of the papal delegate in 1691, and the city thanked the viceroy in a long memorial.

The prisoners were transferred to the prison of the Archbishop of Naples. In 1693 Naples was ravaged by plague and earthquake, and the archbishop saw an opportunity for striking a blow at the philosophers. A solemn ceremony was staged in the cathedral. Before an immense crowd certain of the prisoners were induced to undergo the impressive humiliations of public confession. Over them the archbishop preached a sermon attributing to their wickedness the disasters with which their city had been visited. These calamities showed the necessity of avoiding evil books, especially Marchetti's translation of Lucretius, which had been made with the assistance of the Devil. The sentences of the ecclesiastical court, published on the day before the sermon, had condemned the culprits to ten years' imprisonment and a public abjuration. Their errors were now read out before the great concourse of ladies, cavaliers and populace. They included the propositions that men existed before Adam, that the universe consisted of atoms, that there was no Trinity, no God, no Paradise, no Purgatory, no Hell, that the souls of men were mortal and not essentially different from those of beasts, that the Pope had no rightful authority and that the blood of St. Januarius did not really liquefy in its annual procession through the city. This last was perhaps the most dangerous item of unbelief that could be attributed to anyone in the presence of the populace of Naples. It was emphasized in the sermon.

But the archbishop had gone too far in exercising openly his inquisitorial jurisdiction as a delegate of the Holy Office at Rome. The allegation that confession had been extracted by promises appears to have saved most if not all of the intended victims. The guardians of the constitution again appealed to the viceroy. Permanent deputies were appointed to watch the Inquisition, and two envoys were sent to negotiate with Innocent XII, a Neapolitan, friend of Vico's friendly bishop Rocca, and now refusing to grant the bigots an interdict against his native city. At the same time public right and intellectual freedom were defended in a number of pamphlets by lawyers and men of letters.

In this critical year 1693 Vico was already on terms of friendship with at least one of these writers and soon afterwards with others, whilst among the prisoners of the archbishop were some of his most intimate companions. In Giuseppe Valletta he found almost paternal guidance and encouragement. Valletta, owing to early poverty, had been an advocate, but amassing a large fortune he devoted his money to the pursuits to which he had wished to devote his life. In 1688 he opened to students and writers—of whom he was always a generous benefactor—the choice library which at great expense he had collected. No learned foreigner came to Naples without visiting this library, and the choicest intellectual society of the city was often gathered there. Now in 1693 Vico writes of Valletta in affectionate terms. It was Valletta who persuaded him in that year to publish his poem and to send a copy of it to the great Florentine librarian and scholar Magliabechi. About the same time Vico became a member of one of the most important academies, the *Uniti*, who were a revival or continuation of the *Investiganti*. This accounts, perhaps, for his intimacy with the group around di Capua.

At this time, under favourable auspices, he was entering upon the career of an aspirant for literary fame. His first published poem had been dedicated to Domenico Rocca. His second was probably a deliberate bid for the patronage of a powerful family. It commemorated the exploits of Count Antonio Caraffa, as a statesman the pillar of the Austrian monarchy, as a soldier the bloody suppressor of a Hungarian revolt. Naples was perhaps proud of having given him birth. At least his family was mighty there. His obsequies were celebrated with pomp and among the authors of funereal verse was Vico. It was mere grandiose eulogy. Heaven and Nature and imperial Rome appear in the procession and the young author contributes his own sighs and despair. There is the same background of pessimism as in Vico's real poem. It is when we see the dishing up of what had been a sincere philosophical emotion to adorn such a piece of business as this, that we feel most keenly what a tribute poverty extorts from genius. This poem, too, by Valletta's advice, was sent to Magliabechi. The nephew of the dead general became later one of Vico's pupils, and many years afterwards paid him very tolerably for a biography of his uncle. In 1694 Vico tried the Elector of Bavaria who had helped Sobieski to save Vienna, had himself stormed Belgrade and was now ruling the Netherlands. In due course a brief letter of official thanks reached the young poet. Another poem, on the same Elector's marriage very soon afterwards, was included by its author in a collection printed as late as 1723, which probably means that it was a technically successful example of a sort of composition much practised in those days.

Certainly by 1696, perhaps three years earlier, Vico was well known to several eminent men besides Valletta. The advocate Nicola Caravita made his house the centre of a literary group in which Vico was welcome. Here he became the fast friend of Lucina, generally recognized as one of the most learned and best critics in Naples, but always unsuccessful in competing for a chair at the university. If Vico is to be judged by his friends, there is only one possible view of his mental attitude at this time. In Valletta's library, in the house of Caravita, perhaps of di Capua, and in the meetings of the *Uniti*, he was in habitual association with men who were constantly preoccupied with the promotion of modern ideas and the struggle against the encroachments of the Holy See. No name of a contrary tendency is mentioned in connection with him, either by himself or by anyone else. Valletta and Caravita were leaders in the controversy on the Inquisition. Cristofaro and Galizia, who were perhaps even closer intimates of Vico, had been accused by the papal delegate in 1692 and Cristofaro had been among those arrested. They were well known in the haunts where philosophy was most freely discussed. All Vico's friends of this time were in ill odour with the clergy, a position of which he fought very shy in middle and later life. Whether, as has been suspected he compromised himself in these years among these associates is a question that may never be answered. We shall find in his first philosophical writing more distinct traces of Cartesian doctrine than in the autobiography he will recognize.

He makes in these pages as little as possible of his study of the modern thinkers. He tells us that having heard how Epicureanism, as represented by Gassendi, had become the fashion among the young Neapolitans, he made a study of that philosophy in the poem of Lucretius. "He learned," he says, "that Epicurus, because he denied any generic difference of substance between mind and body, and so, for want of a good metaphysical doctrine, limited his mind, had necessarily to take, as the starting-point for his philosophy, matter already endowed with form and divided into multiform, ultimate parts composed of other parts, which for want of an intervening void he considered to be indivisible. This is a philosophy to satisfy the scant and feeble reasoning powers of boys and young ladies. And though Epicurus had no knowledge of geometry, yet, by a well-ordered deduction, he built up a mechanical physics, a metaphysic entirely sensualistic just like that of John Locke, and a hedonist morality suitable for men living in solitude, as he, in fact, recommended to his disciples. And though, to do him justice, he delighted Vico with his wonderful explanation of the forms of corporeal nature, he excited just as much his ridicule and compassion in the shifts and absurdities he was perforce driven to in order to explain by such principles the operations of the human mind. This reading, therefore, only served to confirm Vico in his Platonic way of thinking." The plain meaning of this passage is, not that Vico came afterwards to see that the atomists were wrong, but that he never thought they were right. But he certainly understates the extent of his intercourse with those "young men of Naples" when he writes that he had "heard of" their Epicureanism; just as he exaggerates his remoteness at Vatolla, during these years, from the intellectual life of Naples.

Nor does he confess that he was influenced by Descartes. "Towards the end of his solitude," he writes, "which lasted nine years, he heard that the physics of Renée Descartes had obscured the renown of all that had gone before, and he ardently desired to become acquainted with it." When he returned to Naples, either for the last time or on one of his earlier visits, he was told that a book he had already read was written by Descartes. This was not true, and it produced in his mind some confusion as to what Descartes really taught. The book was the *Philosophia Naturalis* of Henricus Regius, which name was not, as Vico was told, a pseudonym of Descartes. The work was by a pupil who differed in essentials from his master. Vico saw in it nothing fundamentally different from the doctrine of Epicurus. He started therefore with the mistaken assumption that Descartes was a materialist, whose doctrine of two substances arose from a superficial and disingenuous attempt to reconcile his system with Platonism in order to make it acceptable in certain circles. We shall see reasons for attributing to Vico a definite adhesion to Cartesian principles at no distant time from his final return to Naples. Of this the autobiography says nothing.

As a recreation he read the physics of Robert Boyle But ideas caught casually in such reading between while do sometimes influence a man more than he expects

Vico continued for a long time to reflect on physical subjects; their influence on the first form of his philosophy, as he gave it to the world about twelve years later, is decisive. But this philosophy was permeated throughout with neoplatonism.

Though he only once attended a lecture in the University of Naples, he did not neglect to provide himself with a doctor's degree. He went through the formality of matriculation in 1689, 1690 and 1692, which last was a belated registration for the year 1691–92, perhaps because of a long absence from the city. In 1694 he signed a document as *utriusque juris doctor*. His name does not appear on any list of doctors created in Naples. It has been supposed that like many other impecunious people he took his degree at Salerno, where fees were lower.

CHAPTER V

A VOCATION

FROM the close of his engagement with Domenico Rocca in 1695 or 1696, when he was twenty-seven, Vico lived to the end of his days in Naples. We have a survey of the intellectual condition of Naples at this time as Vico remembered it in 1725. Much as he probably exaggerates his alienation from the existing tendencies, he may well have felt that his own studies had not prepared him to co-operate in them. Nobody now seemed to read the neoplatonists over whom he had spent so much time, and through whose quotations and comments he had familiarized himself with the ideas and historical succession of the ancients. Even Aristotle and Plato were only used as quarries for literary suggestion and by those who wished to make a show of being learned. The scholastic logic was being replaced by Euclid. The throne of philosophy was occupied by Descartes. Algebra was being given a place in education by Caloprese and others. In Vico's opinion its habitual use weakened the powers of the mind to grapple with reality. The old authorities in medicine upon whose principles good work had always been based, had given place to the empiricism and scepticism of di Capua's *Parere*; though Vico does not mention the book he describes the school. In law the "erudite" school, that of the historical critics, from Alciato to d'Andrea, had displaced the old interpreters, and this, says the Vico of 1725, was to the great disadvantage of the forum. With the new movement in poetry he was more in sympathy, for the reasons and with the reservations that have already been noticed. In prose, di Capua had restored the Tuscan grace, but without any sign of the Greek depth or the Roman grandeur. Finally the "latinissimo signor" Tommaso Cornelio had by his classical purism rather deterred than helped the aspirants in Latin prose.

Vico himself was not deterred from emulating Cornelio. He made Latin for the time his principal study. Cornelio had sacrificed his Greek and Italian on the altar of monumental Latin and Vico judged the example worth following. To write Latin as few modern men have written it seemed worth the sacrifice of many conflicting intellectual ambitions. And he gained his object. He attained the power of writing long books in Latin during the evenings of middle life when his room was filled with the conversation of a circle of which he had become the centre. He could write history in the manner of Sallust and address an audience in a style modelled after Cicero. He read his Latin authors now without lexicons and avoided all commentaries, interpreting them by means of themselves, entering into their spirit with what he called a philosophical criticism. He ceased to read Greek and never seriously studied modern languages, though in spite of his professed neglect of French he was no stranger to it, and he was interested in the structure of German. He thought that the study of many languages was not compatible with excellence in any. In coming to this decision he may have remembered the concurrent opinion of Piccolomini. His selection of Latin rather than Italian has been lamented on the ground that, after all, he was destined to write his greatest work in Italian. But with all the ruggedness and Latinism of the *Scienza Nuova*, it is doubtful if a highly conscious cultivation of Tuscan elegance would have given Vico a fitter medium for his immense syntheses and many-sided suggestions. He wrote the *Scienza Nuova* with more thought of the subject than of the language, some of it with astonishing celerity. And so he came to write an Italian difficult indeed and often irregular but strong and pregnant. He was apt to judge Italian writing by Latin or even Greek standards as in his criticism of di Capua to which reference has just been made, and other examples occur in his writings.

In this assiduous cultivation of Latin composition, he was taking a course not altogether irrelevant to his worldly interest. Any public office to which learning was a passport was still likely to involve the production of Latin orations and memorials. But Vico continued to write Italian poetry, though he did so, he says, with "luminous Latin ideas" and in imitation of Latin models. It was with such a poem that he celebrated the nuptials of Vincenzo Caraffa with Ippolita Cantelma. To his connection with the family of Caraffa he thus added another connection which was later on very important in his life. Donna Ippolita, who became a valuable friend, was the centre of a literary circle which met in her house. Burnet had already remarked the way in which French customs, as well as French thought, were making their way in Naples. More than one *salon* now existed in the city. The date when Vico's intimacy with this circle commenced cannot be fixed. At a later period it would be unfair to describe it as patronage, but it was a connection of great worldly advantage. Donna Ippolita was related to the house of Stuart, whilst her own family included the archbishop who had preached the sermon against the philosophers in 1693 and the Duke of Popoli who was soon to have great influence in the state. Her royal descent is not forgotten in Vico's nuptial poem.

Several influential people began to concern themselves about his future. Among these was Gaetano d'Andrea, brother of Francesco d'Andrea. If we regard Francesco as the first important leader of the intellectual revival, it would be interesting to find him in personal relations with Vico, who was its glorious culmination. But the nearest we get to this is a single conversation with Gaetano, who was a member of the aristocratic Theatine order and taught theology and philosophy in the college connected with their sumptuous Renascence church of the Holy Apostles Peter and Paul.

Father Gaetano got into conversation one day with Vico in a bookshop. While they talked of the various collections of Canon Law, he asked him if he was married. Hearing that he was not, he proposed to him to enter the order of Theatines. Vico replied that he had not the necessary qualification of noble birth. He was told that a dispensation could be obtained from Rome. Touched, perhaps, by this urgency from such a man, Vico explained that he had poor and aged parents, who would depend on him for support. D'Andrea, with the worldly good sense so noticeable in his brother's autobiography, remarked that men of letters are rather apt to be burdensome than useful to their families. Vico replied that perhaps it would not be so in his case. "The father closed the conversation by saying, 'That is not your vocation' "; words that Vico was not likely to forget.

Conversations are perhaps the surest parts of an auto-biography that is written from memory. Opinions change gradually, the conditions of life are made up of elements that develop and supersede one another after no apparent chronological ordering, and moods are difficult to recover. But a conversation is a bright spot illuminating a person, a place and the circumstances or views that were dis-cussed. Vico had, it would seem, made as favourable an impression upon the Theatine as years before upon Geronimo Rocca. If we give the softness of youthful genius to the noble but haggard aspect of the portrait we have of his later age, if we consider his openness and enthusiasm, his depth of thought and of philosophical experience and his precocious learning and eloquence, we can see why he received from this distinguished member of an exclusive order so flattering a proposal. On what grounds d'Andrea concluded that Vico was not meant for a man of letters we can only guess. After all, he was right. Vico worried too much over the heart of difficult matters, appeared perhaps pedantic and even ostentatiously so, had perhaps been quietly observed by d'Andrea for some time and registered as more learned than prolific, too awkwardly sincere and cumbrous in his thinking, too much out of the swim generally to make an exception to the general fate of those who try to live by writing. But Vico's own part in the conversation shows him full of adventurous hope, no longer the *disperato* of 1692.

He soon had a considerable encouragement. Santo Stefano, the viceroy, had completed his term of office and was about to return to Spain. Caravita took the lead in promoting the publication of a volume of literary tributes, and Lucina suggested Vico as the writer of the prefatory Latin oration, having, says the latter, "made some trial of the young man." In spite of Lucina's want of worldly success, his eminence as a critic gave him great authority, and he had been waiting for some time to give his young friend an opening, "regretting that the city made no use of him." The oration had to be written at short notice, and some indignity was felt by the other contributors at such an important place among them being given to an unknown novice in literature. They were only pacified by the anonymous issue of the whole collection, but Vico's part in it became known, for he says he began from this point to rise into reputation as a man of letters. It was now that he became acquainted with Caloprese, a philosopher who had devoted himself to the task of educating in the principles of Descartes a number of select youths, among whom were Spinelli, Gravina and Metastasio. To Caloprese Vico says he became very dear. Caloprese called him *autodidascalo*, which Vico paraphrased in the same expression he had used of himself as a schoolboy, *il maestro di se medesimo*. In the same year Charles II of Spain recovered, as far as he ever did recover, from one of the more severe crises in his long life of disease, and Naples put forth a collection of congratulatory addresses to which Vico contributed some verses in Latin, very conventional verses describing the grief of all Nature and especially of the river Tagus at the king's illness, and their joy at his recovery. The most sincere part of the poem is the fear, among the other prognostications of evil to follow the king's death, that a general war for the succession to his dominions could hardly be avoided. This was no very difficult prophecy but a matter of common anxiety. The next year, 1697, died the mother of the new viceroy, who was the Duke of Medinaceli. Vico contributed a Latin oration, which appeared with others in Greek and Italian. It is an epitaph expanded over several pages. Perhaps it is worth noting that he denies the Stoic doctrine of virtue being the only good; the deceased lady's wealth and rank made her virtues beneficial to a large number of people.

Medinaceli came with instructions to conciliate the leading spirits of Naples, especially in the matter of the Inquisition. He was also anxious to appear as a patron of the arts and of literature. The influential character of the circles in which Vico now moved is shown by the fact that, in setting up a literary academy with meetings in his own palace, the viceroy did little more than invest with pomp and prestige the discussions of the group of modernizing philosophers who had hitherto frequented the house of Caravita. The association of government with letters seemed to Vico a restoration of the glorious hopes of the court of Alfonso of Aragon, when Naples was among the chief centres of the Renascence of the fifteenth century. Formal sessions of the Academy of the Royal Palace, or, more briefly, the Royal Academy or *Accademia Medinaceli*, were held twice a month. There they sat in a circle in their armchairs of crimson velvet, the viceroy on an equality with the rest. There sat Vico and as he looked around he saw among others his friends Cristofaro, Galizia and Giannelli, all three stigmatized by the Inquisition in 1692; his friends Valletta and Caravita, leaders of the city in its resistance to the Inquisition, both Cartesians in philosophy; and, in attendance on the viceroy as "general of arms" but without a seat, privileged only to lean on the crimson upholstery, stood the Duke of Popoli, uncle of Vico's patroness Ippolita Cantelmo-Stuart, a man of great influence with Medinaceli. It was in this assemblage that he read his learned discourse on the Feasts of the Romans. It is a piece of pure erudition. In the autobiography he looks back on the Academy of the Palace as a revival of letters, in reaction against the encroachments of modern and physical sciences. He laments that after the departure of Medinaceli the revival came to nothing.

About this time he contracted the principal friendship of his later life. Among the academicians of the palace was Paolo Matteo Doria. He was perhaps the leading mind of the academy. He was by birth a Genoese and was two years older than Vico. Of his reasons for leaving his native city we know at least that some misfortune was connected with it. "Injurious fortune made me an exile," he says in one of his poems. He had amorous adventures; he suffered disappointments; he was the butt of calumny. Gradually he withdrew from society and gave himself almost entirely to science and to letters. He was mathematician, poet, critic and metaphysician. He was among the important writers of his time on education and on the theory of the state. At this time he was regarded as one of the chief Cartesians in Naples. In Vico's life he is of great importance. Vico says he was a *gran cavaliere*, which we may perhaps translate "great gentleman," and a philosopher, and "the first with whom he was able to discuss metaphysics." This last statement is full of suggestion. Was Vico, after all, not so very intimate with Caravita and Valletta? Caravita was probably one of the busiest men in Naples, advocate, professor, academician and controversialist, and with little inclination, perhaps, to discuss metaphysics. Vico, then, was nearly thirty before he found a friend with whom he could discuss the fundamental problems. He represents himself as a Platonist in philosophy and as discovering that his Cartesian friend was also a Platonist without knowing it. Doria later became a leader of the reaction against Descartes, and conducted a slightly acrimonious controversy with Caloprese's pupil Spinelli. If we are right in thinking that Vico was himself Cartesian till about 1709, and yet remained deeply imbued with the neoplatonism he had studied so long and deeply at Vatolla, it will be easy to see how Vico, in his own reaction against Descartes, could regard such a self-deception as possible. The Platonizing Cartesian was a character not unknown to the philosophical life of the time.

In the same year 1697 the secretaryship of the city of Naples fell vacant. Vico competed for it. It was a position for which good Latin was perhaps the principal qualification; it had often been held by men of letters. Vico was unsuccessful, and the discouragement into which he fell very nearly prevented him from competing when, a few months later, a vacancy occurred in the university by the death of the professor of rhetoric. He mentioned this discouragement when Caravita urged him to compete for the chair. Guessing, perhaps, what it was from which the sensitive Vico shrank, Caravita offered, himself, to undertake the formal visits connected with the candidature. Caravita, he says, "gently reproached him for a man of poor spirit," an accusation which Vico readily admitted "where material advantage was concerned."

Until the viceroyalty of Lemos (1610–16) professors had been appointed by the king or the viceroy. Lemos instituted public competitions. These were part of an extensive reorganization by which he sought to enhance the prestige of the university, taking as his model that of Salamanca. The lectures of competitors were delivered before an imposing bench of critics. At their head was the king's chaplain (*Cappellano Maggiore*), who was accompanied to the entrance of the hall by the captain of the university guard, by the master of the ceremonies and by beadles carrying maces. With him sat magistrates of the highest courts of the realm, members of religious orders, and a long array of retired and acting professors. Lemos instituted gorgeous uniforms with a robe of a different colour for each faculty. At their first appearance they were greeted with laughter by an assemblage of Italian ladies and cavaliers to whom Spanish pomp was both unwelcome and ridiculous. But the public in the end grew accustomed to it.

Before such an assemblage, on the 24th of October 1698, Vico and his competitors gave proof of their learning and eloquence in Latin, while the master of the ceremonies turned the hour-glass. Beadles then carried round two urns in which the judges deposited their votes. These had, by the order prescribed in the regulations of Lemos, to be counted by the presiding royal chaplain in the sight of all. In Vico's case the votes were not cast until three months after the competition. He received his appointment to the chair of rhetoric in January 1699.

Though this chair was one of the most poorly paid,

it enabled him to leave the uncomfortable hovel in the street of the booksellers and to rent of the fathers of the Oratory for himself, his father, and his eldest brother, who was a notary, what was at least a house, though a small one, in the *Vicolo dei Giganti*. In the same year he married. His wife, Teresa Caterina Destito, the daughter of a clerk in the criminal court, was unable to sign her name and was obliged to put a cross to the record of their marriage. Though this marriage and the birth of children increased the difficulty of living on his small salary and forced him not only to take private pupils but to write odes and addresses for rich patrons whenever occasion offered, it seems to have provided Vico with domestic happiness. He married for love and spoke of his wife thirty years later "with great feeling and gratitude." The tradition that Caterina was an incapable mother is perhaps worth mentioning, as it has only recently been demolished by the discovery that she has been confused with her daughter-in-law.[5] Vico was an acute observer of children and liked playing with his own. His eldest daughter, at least, and one of his sons, richly repaid the attention he gave to their education.

CHAPTER VI

EARLY TEACHING

VICO was thirty-one when in 1699 he delivered his first inaugural oration in the University of Naples. He retained the chair of rhetoric until 1741, that is, until, overcome with incurable illness, he was succeeded in his seventy-third year by his son. When he first entered on his duties he had still nearly twenty-six years to pass before the publication of his great work, and before writing the autobiography. We have still to follow him for a quarter of a century before he becomes the Vico who wrote the autobiography, whose mood of 1725 colours the story of all that went before. But we are no longer obliged to rely so much upon the autobiography as hitherto. The inaugural orations, which we have yearly for most years from 1699 to 1708, give us much of his thought; he published important works in the years between 1708 and 1725; and we have a correspondence which becomes illuminating towards the end of that period.

He gives us in the autobiography a short account of his own studies at about the time when he became professor; or, more correctly speaking, he inserts the account at that point without explicitly relating it to that time. He had long been occupied with the study of two principal writers, Plato and Tacitus. Like his friends Doria and Caloprese, he read his Plato in Latin. Tacitus, he says, with an incomparably metaphysical mind, contemplates man as he is; Plato contemplates man as he should be. Metaphysical, here as often in Vico, meant psychological. Plato is described as excelling in *sapienza riposta*, which means abstruse, abstract, philosophical and academic wisdom; Tacitus is wise in *sapienza volgare*, which is the wisdom of a historian and statesman as well as that which is implicit in the institutions and customs of a whole people even from the earliest times. This distinction, clearly conceived as part of a system of social and political thought, scarcely belongs to the time of which Vico was writing; at the time when he wrote, it had become self-evident to him and far-reaching.

What Vico derived from Tacitus cannot be adequately understood from a collection of references in his writings. Of the passages quoted many are from the *Germania*, and are adduced principally for the purpose of illustrating Vico's theory of the nature of barbaric and even primitive society. Others relate to the meaning of certain Roman laws, since Tacitus was learned in antiquity. Others illustrate the evolution of Roman institutions under the earlier emperors, and these are the best examples of the kind of wisdom here attributed to the historian, his insight into the psychology of political development. But such references are few. Vico's use of his authors was anything but pedestrian. His knowledge of the Roman constitution was profound, and was certainly in part due to his careful study of Roman historians, in part to his knowledge of jurisprudence. And this understanding of the constitutional history of Rome was the very core of his theory of the history of mankind. One way of regarding Tacitus, which we should expect in a writer of Vico's time, is not very much in evidence in his own work. Tacitus had become to Italian political theorists a substitute for Machiavelli, and Tiberius for

Cesare Borgia, as textbook and model of a statecraft independent of morality. Except for the sentence just quoted, that Tacitus considered man as he is rather than as he ought to be, there is little indication in Vico's published works that he regarded Tacitus in this light. But we possess a series of notes on different passages in Tacitus which Vico seems to have written later on for his pupils. Some of these are certainly comments on statecraft. They show Vico, further, occupied in determining very carefully the exact implication of Latin political terms, a task which was a main part of his "new science."

In telling us that he studied side by side Plato and Tacitus, *sapienza riposta* and *sapienza volgare*, he again strikes the two notes of philosophy and history, whose final accord is to be found in the *Scienza Nuova*, where he will show that history is a temporal development of communities governed by the eternal laws which it is the function of philosophy to discover.

Later, apparently about 1707, he added a third author to the small list of his intensive studies. He discovered Francis Bacon, in whom he found "incomparable wisdom," both of the philosophical and of the popular or historical kind. Neither the Greeks nor the Romans had such an author. What astonished Vico in Bacon was that a single man should see in all branches of knowledge what was entirely wanting as well as what was defective and required to be reformed or extended. The discovery of a writer dealing in this free and penetrating manner with large masses of knowledge was clearly a stimulus to treat the list of sciences as something incomplete, something to be enlarged and supplemented by a new science, a *Scienza Nuova*. It was a great liberation of creative power.

Our chief means of knowing the trend of Vico's thought from 1699 to 1707 are the inaugural orations he delivered in the university. The first was in 1699. It was characteristic of him that, when he needed only to deliver an exhortation to study, expressed in exemplary Latin, he gave philosophical reasons for his counsel, and so provided us with a genetic explanation of his greater works.

The thesis he took for the first oration was "that the knowledge of oneself is for each of us the greatest incentive to the compendious study of the whole circle of knowledge." The philosophical part of the discourse falls into two closely related sections, of which the first is neoplatonic, the second Cartesian. The former consists in developing the implications of the doctrine that the human mind is a simulacrum of Deity. As God is in the universe, the mind is in the body, whole in every part and nowhere contained. God creates Nature; man's mind creates the arts. Because of its divine nature the human mind is fitted to understand the works of God; that is, by knowing itself, to perceive its fitness to survey the whole circle of the arts and sciences and to rise from a knowledge of self to a knowledge of God.

Vico then proceeds to adduce the Cartesian proofs of the possibility of knowing both of our own and of God's existence. They may be called Cartesian proofs in Vico, because although he could have derived the proof of self-existence either from Augustine or from Ficino, and although the ontological proof of the existence of God was originally enunciated by Anselm, the form in which Vico quotes them is the form in which they were stated by Descartes, and an additional proof of God's existence is given which originated with Descartes. Ficino writes, "When the mind doubts of anything, then also is it certain of many things. For it does not doubt that it then doubts."[6] Descartes writes, "Am I not that very being who now doubts of almost everything; who, for all that, understands and conceives certain things?" This is in the *Meditations*, and we read, in the *Discourse of Method*: "From the very circumstance that I thought to doubt of the truth of other things, it most clearly and certainly followed that I was." Vico's words are: "Even if the human mind sticks and altogether doubts concerning all things, it can by no means doubt that it thinks, for this very doubting is thought." The subsumption of doubt under thought is in both Vico and Descartes, but not in Ficino.

With regard to God, Anselm's proof is as follows: "We believe thee (God) to be something than which nothing greater can be thought. . . . And that than which nothing greater can be thought, cannot be in the intellect alone. For if it is in the intellect alone it can be thought to be also in reality; and this is something greater. If therefore that than which nothing greater can be thought is in the intellect alone, then that same thing, than which nothing greater can be thought, is something than which something greater can be thought. But certainly this cannot be. There exists therefore without doubt something than which nothing greater can be thought, and it exists both in the intellect and in reality."[7] Descartes writes: "Returning to the examination of the idea that I had of a perfect Being, I found that existence was comprised in it in the same way as it is comprised in the idea of a triangle that its three angles are equal to two right-angles."[8] Vico's version is, "What is most perfect is endowed with all perfections. . . . It is a perfection to exist. . . . Therefore God exists."

If any further proof is required that Vico took this part of his philosophy from the Cartesian school rather than from any scholastic or neoplatonist writer, it may be noticed that Vico gives, as another proof of the existence of God, that "he perceives the notion of an infinite thing to be in himself; he assumes that there must be as much in the cause as in the thing which is produced by that cause; hence he gathers that this notion of an infinite thing proceeds from a thing which is infinite." This argument originated with Descartes.[9] It is significant that, in summarizing the oration in the autobiography, Vico omitted all the Cartesian arguments. That in so doing he was consciously omitting to record a revolution in his thought should not be rashly inferred. Even when writing the autobiography, he recognized the common element between neoplatonism and Cartesianism. Writing of his conversations with Doria, he says that "what Doria admired as sublime, great and new in Descartes, he himself recognized as old and common among the Platonists." For the purposes of the first oration, the common element was most relevant, the introspective method, the "recalling of the mind from the senses" to study its own contents. The epistemology of neoplatonism, that man knows because his mind is part of the supreme reason, is quite compatible with Descartes' theory of our becoming aware of knowledge by looking within—*Cogito ergo sum*. What is striking is that Vico deliberately chose in 1699 to express these doctrines so as to echo Descartes, and in 1725 seems anxious to disavow the influence of that philosopher entirely. In this oration occurs a singular anticipation of more modern thought. To meet the objection of the man who denies that he is led by Vico's reasoning to a knowledge of God, Vico introduces the conception of unconscious knowledge. The metaphors with which he tries to explain this difficult conception are, first, that of the contents of the mind being like a picture in which the accomplished critic sees many lines and shades unnoticed by the ordinary observer, and, second, that of a top, whose motion is invisible when at its swiftest. This anticipation of the theory of unconscious mind was not systematically developed by Vico.

The inaugural of 1699 was devoted to an investigation of the nature of truth. In that of 1700 Vico discusses the nature of the good. The title of it only indirectly indicates this: "There is no enmity more dire and unrelenting than that which the fool exercises against himself." The fool (*stultus*) is the man who fails to pursue the highest good. The exordium sets forth the strange contrast between the world of Nature, ruled by laws which are never broken, and displaying in the heights and depths of the universe the reign of order and supreme reason, and on the other hand the world of man, always in conflict with himself, a pitiable spectacle of weakness and confusion, admiring virtue but plunged in vice, aiming at happiness but running into misery, greedy of immortality but rotting in utter idleness of which no more can be said than of the nothingness of death itself. Such a spectacle almost tempts the writer to regard mankind as the fruit of some strange seed cast by accident upon earth or to suppose that we are paying the penalty of some antenatal sin.

Rejecting these theories, he pronounces our failure and suffering to be the result of our continual offence against the law of God. That law is twofold, for all else the law that is never broken, for man wisdom (*sapientia*). Imitating the style of the Twelve Tables, he imagines God as issuing the following decrees for man. "Let man be of mortal body and immortal soul. Let him be born for truth and goodness, that is to say for me alone. Let his mind distinguish the true from the false. Let his senses not control his mind. Let him take reason as the principle, the guide and the lord of his life. Let his desires be the handmaids of reason. Let his mind not follow opinion in its judgments but the light of knowledge of self. Let the soul embrace the good, not from inordinate desire but with its rational part. Let man prepare for himself an immortality of fame through the good arts of his spirit. By virtue and constancy let him attain to human felicity. If any be foolish, so as to break these laws through guile or luxury or sloth or even imprudence, he is guilty of treason and must declare war against himself."

Wisdom is the nature of man. If we offend against it we fail to "follow nature," as the Stoics phrase it and Vico after them. Before depicting the war which such offenders must wage against themselves, he brings vividly before his hearers the ordinary battlefield, the leaders bringing out their forces and the fight beginning, the rapid banishment from the faces and minds of the combatants of all that is human, its complete replacement by the bestial passion of killing, the whole mind being intent upon finding in the foeman's body a place where a wound will be deadly; then the devastation, agony and death of the battlefield afterwards; finally the outrage wrought upon matrons, virgins and boys—in face of the altars, in the bosom of their families, while the animalism of the conflict has not yet subsided in the breasts of the victors.

But the war in the soul of him who fails to take reason as the guide of his life is to Vico even more terrible. The arms with which it is waged are the unbridled passions. The rebel cannot overcome the power of conscience. The city which is taken from him is the universe, the vast realm of divine reason. Felicity is the wealth of which he is despoiled. The prison into which he is thrust is his own body. Fortune is the mistress under whose sway he is subjected.

This second oration is connected with the first by the doctrine that the real good which the fool sacrifices is the universe, the city whose walls are "the flaming ramparts of heaven," the city common to God and the wise, the city filled and held together by "that perfect reason by which God does all things and the wise man understands all things." Vico corrects the Stoic doctrine that would make man, by reason of virtue, differ from the gods only in being mortal, to a dictum that is more consistent with catholic orthodoxy; he says that God makes us similar to himself in one thing, virtue, and by this we share celestial as well as human felicity. This virtue consists in equanimity, and a tenour of life always consistent with itself; it is only possible through the knowledge (*scientia*) of things, and through practical wisdom (*prudentia*), through knowing what is certain, doing what is right, and so, by knowledge, contemplating God, and, by action, imitating him. Wisdom consists in living in the mind, approaching God through it by investigating "causes of things." The sage will withdraw the soul as far as possible from the body and its concerns, will converse as much as may be with his better and diviner part, his mind, and will have as little as possible to do with that other "querulous and fragile" nature of his. Like the Stoics, Vico sees the body, fame, wealth, as outside us; they are servants of another law. There are signs in the second oration of a preoccupation with subjects, books and schools of thought other than those which had occupied him a year earlier. He is now especially inclined to use the language of the Stoics. But in the basis of their thought the two orations are the same, the dualism of mind and Nature, the similarity of the divine and human mind.

No inaugural oration was delivered in 1701. At the time when these orations were usually spoken the city was, in that year, a scene of confusion and alarm. In 1700 the event for which the statesmen of Europe had for years been trying to prepare, the death of the Spanish king, let loose the war which Vico regarded as the modern counterpart of that between Rome and Carthage. In Naples the great majority of the people acquiesced in the viceroy's proclamation of Philip V. But there were undercurrents of hostility. The laxer monks feared the French religious discipline; discontented nobles expected favour from an Austrian prince; and patriots preferred an archduke who would be king of Naples alone to Philip V who was king also of Spain. Among the small number of idealists whom this desire for national independence beguiled into desperate association, were Vico's pupil Zaverio Rocca, and Pansutus, a young man whose love of letters, without wealth or rank, had procured his admission to the viceregal academy, where he won the liking and respect of Vico.

In the councils of the plotters the more unscrupulous leaders predominated. A design to assassinate Medinaceli failed, but the prisons were broken open, and the streets became the scene of civil war and incendiarism during two days and nights. Vico was one of two writers appointed to write the official history. Neither's work was accepted; Vico's *de Parthenopea Conjuratione*, almost certainly on account of its monumental impartiality, was not printed until 1836. No one can read it without seeing that its author, as was to be expected of him, once entrusted with the task, did his best to rival Sallust or Tacitus. The description of the cavern where the conspirators stored their arms could only have been written by one who had stood within its gloom. This graphic quality extends to the characters and the events. Truth to life involved a distinct picture of the faults as well as the merits of government, and whilst justice is meted to those who plotted from a sinister ambition, it is also accorded to those who joined them from finer motives and met their fate with dignity. Vico had little sympathy with turbulence and revolution, and feudal anarchy was to him the most hateful of political disorders, as he showed clearly in his description years afterwards of the wars in Hungary. But he had much sympathy with the class of men who toil, and it pleased him to record that among the crowd of desperate beings who held justice at bay

through two fearful nights were none whose hands were
hardened by labour. When the danger was past, ordinary
citizens felt a new sense of the blessings of order and
government, a revived love of the city which had been
in peril.

Soon afterwards Medinaceli was recalled, and was
succeeded by the Duke of Ascalona, the last of the
Spanish viceroys. Medinaceli was pursued with defamatory writings by the monks of Naples. "It is much to
his honour," wrote Vico, "to have been grievous to such
men." Philip V visited Naples in 1702, distributing
largesses and honours and remitting taxation. He received
a free gift of money, a statue and loyal addresses. The
wish of the people was for a king who would reside
among them. Vico, by order of the Duke of Ascalona,
wrote a panegyrical oration. It is of no more significance
than any other formality of the occasion. Its author's
whole life was a wrestling with the angel of difficult and
sublime truth. His history of the late rising was too true
to be published. But the professor of rhetoric was, it
would seem, also the public orator; so Vico is found
telling Philip the Bourbon that he was the greatest being
on earth and that in his royal body he was more beautiful
than a beautiful woman. In 1707 the Austrians marched
in, and Naples ended its long membership of the Spanish
empire. The traitors of yesterday became the martyrs
of to-day. In a polite letter the professor of rhetoric was
requested by Count Daun, the new viceroy, to write
inscriptions for the tombs of Capece and Sangro, two
of the leaders executed in 1701. Though they had sought
to prevent Naples from being governed by the greatest
being on earth, Vico wrote their inscriptions. It was all

so much a matter of course that he commented in his autobiography on the compliments which exalted persons paid him on account of the excellence of his Latin. A great man's mind is, after all, like the glory of pictures and poems, in the style of his age.

In 1702[10] he delivered his third inaugural oration. It was precisely such a sermon as might have been expected from an associate of the principal Cartesians of Naples, from a man who sympathized with the efforts of Lionardo di Capua and his friends to clear away anti-scientific prejudice and to prepare the young to receive with open mind the methods and results of new research. The text is that the republic of letters ought not to be infested with self-seeking and vain pretence. All nature save man is bound by law; man only, to his sorrow, has a free will; of all the evils to which this leads the worst are those resulting from the abuse of the highest things, the interests of the mind. The two earlier orations had dealt with the individual aspirant towards intellectual perfection, or with his opposite. The third, which Vico calls a "practical appendix" to the other two, introduces the claims of a community, the republic of letters. The examples are full of suggestion as to the course of Vico's thoughts. He attacks above all the self-satisfied sciolist who with easy criticism belittles the greatest thinkers of all time, from Zeno, Democritus and Plato to Descartes. He tells the story—for which parallels could be found in life—of the man who made every excuse for refusing to look through a microscope; the real reason was that he held the traditional belief of the nerves being rooted in the heart, and this belief he did not wish to lose. This is the obscurantist in science. The charlatan in philosophy takes refuge in occult qualities to conceal his ignorance of causality. But we meet also the bigot of the new philosophy, who pretends to have a mathematical proof of certain propositions of Descartes which candid disciples like Malebranche have abandoned. Another kind of impostor is seen in the sham scholar who, on a comparatively short acquaintance, claims an intimate appreciation of ancient authors where the greatest critics confess themselves on uncertain ground. Pursuing this case into the region of the Semitic languages, Vico shows a thoroughly critical attitude towards translations of the Old Testament, and gives reasons for distrusting both the Septuagint and the Vulgate. The ideal throughout is of a generous amenity in dealing with the merits of others, a magnanimous humility confronting with courage and industry the immense difficulty and uncertainty of truth, and a wise and honest receptivity for new knowledge and better method.

The fourth oration was pronounced, as Vico, though very questionably, tells us, in the year 1704. In it the social tendency of the third is still further developed; the community to be served is now not the republic of letters but the whole body politic. "He who would reap from his studies the greatest advantages (*utilitates*) combined with honour (*honestate*), should be educated for the commonwealth, for the common good of citizens." The most philosophical part of the oration relates to the distinction between *honestum* and *utile*. Vico objects to the distinction. For him the highest good is the possession of truth; and the reward of virtue, as for Spinoza, is virtue itself. For the purpose of argument he admits that in material things it is not at first sight obvious that what is good and honourable is always advantageous. He finds, however, in the social synthesis an identification of reward and virtue in the highest pursuits. Whoever with his knowledge serves other men is rendered thereby the more productive intellectually, and so shares the enhancement of being which he confers on others. The Stoics and Epicureans have a philosophy suitable for hermits, but the necessary sphere of all the virtues is the service of the community. Vico sketches for the public-spirited student a career of promotion and honour, as if even external rewards, though they should not be the aim, were the acceptable consequences of merit. At the summit of the ladder he places true glory, for him who finds his joy in the work itself and in the service of others. It was the only reward which, in his lifetime, awaited the speaker himself.

What was the political community to which his hearers were to devote their lives? The praise of Naples affords several eloquent paragraphs in Vico's writings. But he shows no desire to change its quiet and secondary position in the world of states. He combines the claims of Italy, Naples and the Spanish empire so as to show the special advantage of this particular complex of loyalties and histories. The young Neapolitans are to congratulate themselves that they live in a Christian country, the seat of the head of the church, that their city is one of the largest in the world, thanks to the greatness of their ancestors both in peace and in war and to the wonderful constitution bestowed upon it by its founders in the heroic age of the most remote antiquity. Naples, moreover, having the same king as Spain, is joined by a firm alliance with the most extensive empire on earth.

The ideal of public service upheld in this oration is

that of the jurisconsult, who, having held the most honourable offices, places his experience gratuitously at the service of his fellow citizens, and so assists in developing the institutions of his country. The praise of the Neapolitan constitution is as curious as that bestowed by Burke upon the unreformed constitution of England. That Vico should attach so much importance to the founders of the state shows that he had not yet conceived his theory of the gradual self-creation of every people.

In the oration of 1705 he undertakes to prove that the political and military power of a state is in proportion to the intellectual cultivation of the citizens. In the view of the speaker, wars are justified when they vindicate the Law of Nations, and are necessary because between nations the sanctions which enforce law among fellow citizens do not exist. The cultivation of military excellence for its own sake, as in Sparta, is as unjustifiable as the devastating conquests of barbarians. The only states which can possibly understand the true aims of war are those where a conception exists of the nature of civilization and of the rights of the community of nations. A knowledge of jurisprudence befits a commander because it is his high and solemn function, if victorious, to apply the principles of justice in a situation in which he is the only judge with power to enforce his decisions. Civilized nations alone can permanently wage successful war, since war is a progressive science requiring a high level of intellectual cultivation; this intellectual cultivation, on the other hand, promotes the social morality on which the true fortitude and stability of a community depend.

Meanwhile the war of the Spanish Succession had been raging in Germany and in northern Italy. The tide of success, from 1704 in the former country, from 1705 in the latter, had run steadily against the French dynasty, and, though Philip V was not to lose Spain, he did in 1707 lose Naples, which hitherto, except for the tumult of 1701, had escaped forming part of the theatre of devastation. The Austrian occupation of Naples took place in 1707 practically without resistance.

In Vico's sixth oration,[11] delivered in the October of that year, three months after the change of government, there is no mention of the important event. The theme of this oration recalls that of the first. The point of view is changed. It is not now the divine character of the human mind, but "the knowledge of corrupt human nature" which "invites us to study the complete circle of the liberal arts and sciences." Corrupt human nature is that of man after his expulsion from Eden, though the lowest point in the fall is reached in the scattering of the race after the adventure of the tower of Babel. The contrast between fallen man in his condition of isolation, as an individual devoid both of all social virtue and of all intellectual culture, and man in the state of what is already, in this oration, denominated *humanitas* has begun to shape for Vico the fundamental problem of history. The nature, origin and evolutionary laws of *humanitas*, its philosophy and its history, were later to be the principal subject of his studies.

"The knowledge of corrupt human nature," to complete the title of this oration, "also determines the true, easy and unvarying order in which they (the liberal arts and sciences) are to be acquired." In demonstration of this the orator first classifies the arts and sciences according to their subject-matter, and then allots to each its place in a scheme of education according to the order in which the faculties ripen. The whole sphere of wisdom embraces first the knowledge of divine things, then prudence that is concerned with human things, and finally the truth and dignity of discourse. Divine knowledge is of two kinds, that which regards Nature and that which regards God; or, as Vico puts it here, that in which Nature is God (natural science) and that in which God is Nature, this last being divine knowledge properly so called. In the broad distinction of human and divine knowledge, so as to include natural knowledge under the head of divine knowledge, we see a repetition of the demarcation in the first oration between God the maker of Nature and the human mind as the god or creator of the arts. Of natural knowledge there are two branches, mathematics, consisting of truths of form and number wherein all men agree, and physics, the realm of causation, wherein is much dispute. Divine knowledge in the narrower sense is knowledge of God and of the human mind, being divided into theology and metaphysics (psychology). Returning to the broader distinction between divine and human wisdom, the latter is moral when the individual is regarded as a man, civil when he is regarded as a citizen, and both moral and civil prudence, when conformed to the Christian religion, are moral theology; moral and civil prudence and moral theology all contribute to jurisprudence, which is neither art nor science. Finally, as distinguished from divine and human wisdom, there is the wisdom of discourse, and our professor of rhetoric always brings this human power into prominence. With the truth of speech is concerned logic; with its fitness or worthiness rhetori-

and poetry. Wisdom in each of its three branches (science, art and prudence) is served by history, in the Baconian meaning of history as a collection of illustrative examples.

Man's fallen nature determines the order in which alone studies can be fruitfully pursued. In childhood memory, in youth imagination, in manhood reason is the predominant faculty. Languages should therefore be taught first, and the most important of these are Greek, Latin and Hebrew, Greek as containing the greater stores of learning, Latin as more commonly used, Hebrew for religion. To exercise, and at the same time restrain and curtail the imagination, an adolescent should study geometry. This science promotes the purification of the soul from matter, which is the essential progress of the soul towards reason, a doctrine in which every neoplatonist would have agreed with Vico. The end of study is not, as men dominated by ambition suppose, the knowledge of the arts and sciences themselves. They are means and not ends. The true end is wisdom and virtue, and to approach God by means of the mind.

It would be impossible to claim rank for Vico as an original philosopher on the evidence of the inaugural orations. They show him to have possessed philosophical scholarship. They show him to have been no mere indiscriminate student of the philosophies of others. He is eclectic. He applies conceptions neoplatonic in origin but modified by Christian beliefs to the philosophies of his own day. The modern philosophy by which he is most influenced is that of Descartes. This is perhaps the reason why he never published these lectures, for his attitude to the philosophy of Descartes was profoundly altered within two years of their completion.

CHAPTER VII

A TREATISE ON METHOD

THE change of rulers in 1707 made little difference to the essential life of Naples. Two centuries of intimate connection with Spain were ended. An Austrian general was viceroy, and then, after a few months, a Venetian cardinal, giving occasion by his presence for special pomp at Vico's inaugural oration for 1708. Amplified and revised, the lecture was published in 1709. The stimulus to this first effort of original thought came from Bacon. Its object, says Vico, was the discovery of a new field of knowledge such as might have been indicated by the author of the *Advancement of Learning*. In viewing scientific method from the three standpoints of instruments, helps and the end for which they are applied, he is closely following Bacon.[12]

Among helps (*adjumenta*) he reckons printing, universities and collections of masterpieces. His idea of instruments is derived from the connection between *instrumentum* and *instructus*. He thought philologically. "Whoever," he says, "properly instructed, approaches the study of any art or science, approaches it properly and in order."[13] The common instrument of all the arts and sciences is the new criticism, *nova critica*, the method of Descartes. In this, modern thinkers have a criterion of absolute truth.

But the general tenour of this treatise on the method of modern studies shows Vico gradually separating himself from the Cartesians. Without attacking as yet the fundamental principles of the school, he was reacting against almost all its tendencies. He enumerates its defects. The first is its disregard for everything except the absolute truth of which it is the criterion. It neglects all civil wisdom and eloquence, all that depends upon vicissitude and possibility, the judgment of the statesman, the behaviour of senates and peoples. Purely critical, it leads to a neglect of what the ancients called topical art, through which the mind is enriched by seeking out all aspects of a question. The second defect is its tendency to apply the geometrical method to all the sciences. Geometry affords purely formal truth. "We demonstrate geometry because we make it." The full meaning of this first enunciation of Vico's fundamental thought must be examined later, but it means at least that analytic and deductive reasoning puts nothing into our minds that was not there before. Vico is all for Baconian induction as against the syllogism. A third objection to the Cartesian influence relates to literature, especially for Italians. It was not by chance that this philosophy arose in France whose language is so well furnished with abstractions, so inapt for the metaphor and the needs of a rich and moving poetry, so different in these respects from Italian. "Minds," says Vico, "are formed by the character of a language and not languages by the minds of those who speak them."

Vico's theory of poetry at this time is certainly influenced by the Cartesians; he writes, for example, that the severe lessons of the philosopher are rendered delightful by the poet. But he is already coming to feel differently, above all to lay more stress on imagination and memory, which the critical method weakens. On the other hand, physical science enlarges the resources of the poet. Poetic language often consists in replacing a merely denotative expression like "thunderbolt" by an explanatory one like "fire struck from the clouds," or "night" by "earth's shadow." In 1707 Vico had recommended geometry as the logic of youth because it tended to weaken and exhaust imagination. He now looks to it to cultivate and develop that faculty. He is already facing the problem of the superiority of the poets of early and barbarous times. His temporary solution is found in the tendency of later writers to imitate their predecessors. The only way to excel these is for the poet or artist to study life and nature for himself. Vico's later solution will occupy us in another chapter.

The passages on religion and jurisprudence abound with pregnant suggestions. The Christian Church has laid the greatest emphasis on preserving belief unaltered. In the pagan religions there was a continual development of myth but a stable element in ceremonial; hence the importance of approaching their historical study from the point of view of rites and formulas. In the history of Roman law he explains the rigidity and religious, esoteric nature of the early rules, and their successive adaptation, with the development of democracy, first by fictions, then by legislation, to the requirements of equity and policy. We are reminded in these pages far more often of the historical methods of the nineteenth century than of the treatment of the same subject, for instance, by Gravina, in this field the greatest of Vico's contemporaries.

The publication of this work gained for its author the friendship of a colleague who had hitherto remained aloof from him. The generous but misanthropic d'Aulisio had drawn upon himself the wrath of all the progressive party by a facetious poem on di Capua.[14] He was himself progressive in his historical method of teaching law. But in all else he was reputed a great opponent of innovation. Vico had come to the university as a friend and associate of the friends of di Capua. On this account D'Aulisio had avoided him. But he read and approved the treatise on method. He took an early opportunity at some public ceremony of asking Vico to sit by him. He complimented him "as a man who did not study by turning over indexes, but as one whose every page might give occasion to others to write volumes." D'Aulisio was a great opponent of the Cartesians, largely because of their neglect of the erudition in which he found Vico so rich. Vico was deeply touched by this recognition from one "otherwise so stern and scant of praise," and he felt in d'Aulisio "a singular greatness of spirit." The two contracted "a very close friendship."

CHAPTER VIII

THE MOST ANCIENT WISDOM OF THE ITALIANS

(1) *A Theory of Knowledge*

A YEAR after publishing the treatise on method, Vico gave to the world under the title at the head of this chapter the book which he afterwards called his metaphysics. The title is due to his fantastic method of exposition. He assumed that very early in its history the Latin language had been made by disciples of Etruscan and Greek teachers a repository of profound philosophy, and especially of that of Zeno of Elea. He therefore elaborates his own metaphysics as if he were examining the meaning of certain Latin words. On similar lines he had produced a small treatise on medicine which has entirely disappeared; it was dedicated to his new friend d'Aulisio. He represents himself as discussing the subject with other friends in the house of Doria, and as deriving suggestions from the writings of Bacon and Plato on mythology and on the origins of language. He had been reading *The Wisdom of the Ancients* and the *Cratylus*.

The first section of the first chapter starts with the assertion that among the Latins *verum* and *factum* were convertible terms. He thus announced without warning and without proof the cardinal doctrine of his epistemology, the identity of truth or knowledge with creative action. A great many writers have remarked that whoever has made a thing knows it.[15] Vico proclaims that nobody knows anything he has not made. Throughout the

Christian centuries it was inevitable that omniscience should be ascribed to God, who had created all things. As an incidental observation Vico's criterion of truth had occurred to a number of thinkers, but not as the basis of a philosophical system. In his treatise on method he had written that we can demonstrate geometry because we make it. The geometrical point, whose movement is the cause of all the geometrical figures, does not exist except as a figment of the human mind. It is the same with the unit whose multiplication gives us arithmetic. The point and the arithmetical unit are abstractions. Mathematical knowledge is thus made by man. It is not a knowledge of realities like God's knowledge of the created universe, but of man-created fictions. In proportion as human knowledge contains anything more than such abstractions or unreal entities it is less certain; mechanics less than arithmetic, physics than mechanics, moral science less certain than physics.

Metaphysical readers will perceive at once, what was observed by Jacobi when Goethe gave him a volume of Vico, the resemblance of this teaching to Kant's theory of the *a priori* element in perception. Vico again anticipates Kant when he applies the criterion in favour of the experimental method of Bacon or Galileo.[16] He who makes an experiment creates the conditions under which he makes his observations. "The reason only sees that which she produces herself according to her own plan." Vico applies the same doctrine to ethics. "The good and the true are convertible in the sense that if any truth is known it owes its being to the mind by which it is known." God, who made all things, "saw that they were good." In 1720 he will write that "what is not from God is nothing."[17] The generation of Leibnitz and Vico, like that of Milton and Spinoza, was much exercised about the problem of evil, about justifying the ways of God to man. Spinoza solved it by denying the objective nature of evil, Leibnitz by limiting the power of God. These are the only possibilities; and Vico, to whom we must not look for consistency, adopts both, at least by implication. The logical consequence of the passages just quoted is the unreality of evil. Later in the same work, however, in a chapter on "Fortune" he compares God to a statesman who, to ensure the general prosperity, must inflict injury on individuals. Another implication of his epistemology, and Vico does not shrink from it, is the impossibility of proving the existence of God, since to do that were to claim to be the maker of God. The close of his chapter "on causes" shows him struggling with this agnostic result and taking refuge in poetry to transcend his own logic: "Those people are to be condemned for impious curiosity who try to prove God by *a priori* reasoning. It amounts to a claim to make themselves the gods of God and to deny the God they seek. The clarity of metaphysic truth is like that of light, which we only know by means of things that are opaque. If you look long and intently at a barred window which admits light into a house, you will transform your line of vision into an altogether opaque body. You will seem to see not light but luminous bars. Metaphysic truth has the same kind of brightness, being confined within no boundary, nor having any form by which it can be discerned, since it is the infinite principle of all forms; physical things are opaque; they have form and boundary and in them we see the light of metaphysical truth."

(2) *The Attack on Descartes*

Having thus attained his own theory of knowledge, Vico sees his way to an attack upon the fundamental doctrine of Descartes. The latter's dictum, "I think, therefore I am," does not give us the knowledge of our own existence but merely a consciousness of it. For this no philosophy is needed. Plautus, in the Amphytrio, puts equivalent language into the mouth of the slave Sosia. Mercury in this play takes the form of Sosia and meets the real Sosia, whose first impulse is to doubt his own identity. But he concludes that, when he thinks, he is certainly the same man he has always been. Vico misquotes slightly so as to make him say "When I think I certainly am and always was." But this consciousness no sceptic will repudiate. Even the deceitful god, the *genius fallax* Mercury, cannot cheat him out of it, though he be a common, ignorant fellow like Sosia. True knowledge is something general and formal, giving us the ground of a thing and how it comes to be. To have true knowledge of my own being I must have created myself.

The causes of things are truths in the mind of God. These Vico calls *genera*. A genus is a kind of universal, but not an abstract idea. It is an archetypal "form" in the neoplatonic sense. To satisfy his philological caprice Vico remarks that the ancient language of Latium gave *genera* the same meaning as *formae*. General ideas in the sense of abstract ideas have indeed their use as the dynamic of ratiocination. By emptying the mind of particular forms they prepare it to receive other particular forms. But this is only one more recognition of our inability to know things intuitively and immediately, with the interior and full knowledge of them as they really are and as God knows them. The causal, creative power of God is infinite behind every creation of the finite. It is the same in creating an ant as in creating the universe. The sages of religion can mount up in contemplation from a flower to God.

(3) *"Metaphysical Points"*

Vico's theory of creation brings us to his famous "metaphysical points." This doctrine is simply an attempt to imagine the action of God, whom we do not know, by that creative knowledge of unreal entities which is all that our minds possess. We create geometrical figures by means of the geometrical point. By an ingenious analogy Vico assumes God to create real things, the whole universe, by means of metaphysical points. God is the sum of all perfection and contains the principle of everything. He is not in motion and he is not extended, but in him are the principles, powers or causes of motion and extension. The problem was to relate the unmoved, unextended, infinite with the finite, moving objects which occupy space in the created universe. The intermediary conceived by Vico is what he calls "first matter" (*prima materia*) and its quality is conation. We have therefore three realities, God, first matter, and extended body. To these belong respectively *quies*, *conatus* and *motus*. Conation is the same behind all degrees of movement; it knows nothing of more or less; it is infinite. It is the exercise of creative power but it is neither creator nor created. "First matter," in which conation takes place, consists of metaphysical points, but it has none of the qualities of matter. Vico's theory must not be confused with any sort of atomic theory. "First matter" has none of the qualities of matter, being neither extended nor divisible nor capable of motion; and conation is to be carefully distinguished from movement, though every movement results from it.

Motion is the quality of extended bodies. It cannot be communicated from one body to another because it cannot be separated from the body in which it is. For one body to receive the motion of another body the two bodies would have to occupy the same space. All bodies are always in motion, and the cause of motion is never anything but conation, which is the action of the un-extended, timeless, immovable, infinite being of God. An event in the physical world preceding another may be called its occasion; its cause is always in the metaphysical world, in God. It has been rightly objected that the difficulty of conceiving creation is not really obviated by calling it conation or by the analogy of metaphysical points, which, in the plural or in the singular, fail equally to represent the relation between a creative, infinite One and the many, finite objects created; nor does it appear how motion arose from that which cannot be conceived as having anything in common with a universe in which motion exists.[18] It has not escaped students of Vico that his treatment of causation anticipates that of Hume, as his theory of knowledge foreshadows that of Kant. But the work of these philosophers, in order to attain its true significance and life as philosophy, required its peculiar place in the history of thought. Vico's thoughts on these subjects remained therefore mere broken lights of the philosophic future.

There is a close connection between the metaphysical points and the theory that *verum* is *factum*. Vico's doctrine of knowledge and his doctrine of being were one vision. God alone has true knowledge of real things; God alone is their cause. The only way by which man can have a similitude of the real knowledge which God creates, together with its object, through metaphysical points, is to imitate these points by the conception of geometrical points. Vico had such a strong sense of the unity of Being that he tended to see all things as one in the mind of God. Only in the whole and entire truth as it is in God could he see reality, since a knowledge of parts is a knowledge of things as they are not, an anatomy which treats the living truth as dead. Compared with God nothing else is. God is; man merely exists. God being the only truth and truth being identical with fact, there is no fact, no thing created or done, save in the mind of God. His critics saw here a form of pantheism. He defended himself, though not very successfully, by the vague notion of degrees of reality. Though created things, bodily or mental, are not substance as God is substance, they partake of substance. Nor will he admit that his virtual agnosticism in metaphysics affects religion. The metaphysical truth which our own minds are incapable of discovering is given in revelation. The possibility, on his principles, of revelation he nowhere examines. But that by reason of it the ancient Hebrews were in possession of an esoteric wisdom superior to all others he does not doubt. He sees in the Mosaic definition of deity, "I am," a confirmation of his own doctrine of God as the only true Being.

CHAPTER IX

THE LIFE OF CARAFFA

THOUGH Vico's chair at the university was one of the humblest and worst paid and he was obliged to increase his income by private teaching, the social circle in which he lived was interesting and appreciated his value. So far as we know he never lost a friend except by death. He had recently contracted a close friendship with Aulisio. With Doria, who published his own political theory in 1710, he was in very intimate relations; he commemorated their intercourse in the dedicatory epistle to the *de Antiquissima*. Valletta, who died in 1714 at the age of seventy-eight, was to the last the active benefactor of the group of writers to which Vico belonged. "They all," we read, "resorted to Giuseppe Valletta, either to show their productions or to get advice and direction from him, or to use his rare books. People came from every quarter to hear the literary news which he received from almost every province."[19] The same author mentions Vico among those who visited Valletta frequently.

It was in 1710, a little before the publication of the *de Antiquissima*, that Vico became an Arcadian. That famous society of which Gravina had been one of the founders at Rome some twenty years earlier, was continuing under difficulties its task of purifying, by example and criticism, the literature and especially the poetry of Italy from the excesses of the seventeenth century. It had colonies in various cities, including Naples. A dispute had arisen among its leaders. Gravina was the most generous of men in his encouragement and assistance to youth. His adoption of Metastasio, whom he sent to be educated by Caloprese, is only the best known example. But he was not always easy to co-operate with. He made enemies by his "superbly frank and biting modes of speech."[20] The quarrel in Arcadia came to a head in 1711 with Gravina's exclusion. Vico's admission belongs to 1710. The "chief shepherd" was the Abate Mario Crescimbene.

Vico was then known as the author of the *de Nostri Temporis Studiorum Ratione*, but the Arcadians wanted him as a poet. He was invited to send a poem which might be included in an anthology of the works of living poets and serve as an example. He replied in a letter of thanks, mentioned that he hoped, as soon as he had recovered from an illness, to publish his book on metaphysics, and sent a poem. It was a sonnet he had written many years before. He excused this to Crescimbene by saying that "these amenities had passed away, with the serene years of his life." The sonnet had appeared in print, together with poems by others, in 1701. It was a love poem, perhaps written at Vatolla, perhaps addressed to a living woman. We do not know. It begins:

> Donna bella, e gentil, pregio, ed onore
> Chiaro immortal dell' amoroso regno . . .

And it concludes:

> O degna, che l'etate
> Io consumi per voi tutta in sospiri.

The chief Arcadian at Naples was the advocate Avitabile,[21] a Latin and Italian poet, also a professor of theology and philosophy. It was apparently by his means that several distinguished Neapolitans were admitted to Arcadia in 1710. The first was Valletta. Another was Vico's early friend Giuseppe Lucina, that scholar of vast erudition in Greek, Latin and Tuscan, who could never obtain a professorial chair. A third was the Duchess of Bruzzano, Ippolita Cantelmo-Stuart of the royal house of Scotland. It was at Vico's instance that Avitabile requested her admission. This lady was already among Vico's inner circle of friends. She was godmother to his daughter Angela, who was born in 1709. He had written as early as 1696 a canzone in celebration of her marriage with Vincenzo Caraffa, Duke of Bruzzano. Vico wrote later of her great dignity of manner, her singular loftiness of spirit and her great thoughts. Avitabile, who was not well acquainted with her, waited until Vico had recovered from his illness before paying the ceremonial visit offering her admission into Arcadia; he desired Vico to accompany him. It was at Vico's house that Ippolita met the other remarkable poetess of Vico's acquaintance, Angela Cimini, herself the leader of a literary social group. A third poetess among Vico's friends was Eleonora Barbapiccola, the particular friend of his daughter Luisa, who, as she grew up, showed precocious poetical talent herself.

Hadrian Caraffa, Duke of Traetto, who had been one of Vico's pupils, was a nephew of the general who had risen so high in the Austrian service and left so terrible a memory of his rule in Hungary. Marshal Caraffa's obsequies had been performed with great ceremony in Naples in 1693 and Vico had contributed verses. The nephew had in his possession a large quantity of documentary material for a biography which, in 1714, he asked Vico to write. Over this task two years were spent, one in arranging the materials, the other in composition. It was no mere compilation but a historical study of the Hungarian wars, involving an intense labour of construction and written at great length in Latin. Vico composed it amid the noise of his family and the conversation of his friends during a time of physical suffering and domestic anxiety.

Written for the nephew of its subject, it could hardly be expected that the *de Rebus Gestis Antonii Caraphaei* should be severely critical of the marshal's conduct. It was written to a great extent from his own papers. Vico can scarcely be said to have been in possession of the Hungarian point of view. On the other hand, the narrative derives its unity rather from the Hungarian revolt than from the character of Caraffa, and, though the statecraft and generalship of the latter receive careful treatment, the personality which seizes the imagination of the reader is that of the romantic rebel Toekoeli. Vico prefaced the work with an enthusiastic passage on the glory of Naples which had retained her independence through so many centuries; but in the Hungarian insurrection he saw merely the ambition of feudal magnates whose turbulence and recklessness imperilled at a critical epoch the frontiers of Christendom towards the menacing world of Islam. Moreover, the incompatibility of feudalism with civil liberty was one of his clearest convictions.

For the larger issues of the near Eastern situation his historical and ethnological vision was wide and definite. He saw Hungary, and more especially the mountains and fastnesses of Transylvania, as the battlefield whose possession opened the way on the one hand to Vienna and all central Europe, on the other to Constantinople and the whole of Turkey's Balkan empire. He surveyed the vast, half-barbarous North where the Slavonic dialects had become coextensive with a wide commerce in the products of boundless plains, whilst Latin was still a spoken language in the intercourse of Teuton, Magyar and Slav. Beyond were the restless hordes of central Asia and the Tartar empire of the Grand Cham. The hosts of Islam, the vicissitudes of fortune that make up the history and romance of Eastern lands, the rise and fall of sultans or viziers have, in Vico's pages, no lack of oriental colour.

Across the plains of Hungary the contest sways from Vienna to Transylvania and from Belgrade to the Carpathians. The story embraces that momentous period during which the conquests of Suleyman the Magnificent were lost for ever to the Empire of the Sultans and the situation established at the close of the middle ages gave place to that which was inherited by the nineteenth century. The persons of the drama are the Hungarian and Transylvanian rebels, Toekoeli with his heroic wife Helen Zrini and the lethargic Apaffy—all the characters of Jokai's romance; and in wider orbits move the potentates of the Germanic empire and the Polish kingdom: Max Emmanuel of Bavaria who took Belgrade, Charles of Lorraine, Lewis of Baden, Eugene of Savoy and Sobieski himself, the saviour of Vienna. Active among these, but always, until near the end, in a subordinate position, is the perpetual Mentor of the Emperor, Antonio Caraffa, the Ulysses of the epic, Vico's countryman.

In spite of the theorizing bent of his own mind, Vico writes entirely in the spirit of the ideal historian he had imagined in his treatise on method. He sees clearly that political and military events require political and military explanation, that details compose the chain of causality and that coincidence is of supreme importance. His presentation is thoroughly concrete. But this does not imply the absence of philosophy; Tacitus was for him the most philosophical of historians. Though the subject of the biography was a model of statecraft, the biographer gives something far deeper than a study of policy. This is nowhere more remarkable than in passages in which it is obvious that he has fresh in his memory the writings of Machiavelli.

In his *Discourses on the first Ten Books of Livy*, Machiavelli says, "men work either by necessity or by choice," and "there is most virtue where choice governs least."[22] It is clear from the context that he means either the hardships of a geographical situation forcing men to effort, or the discipline imposed by law to the same end. Vico, in the second chapter of the life of Caraffa, writes that "good counsels, which are the chief agent in bringing about the felicity of a state, are themselves enforced by necessity, with which virtue is almost always associated, for by the operation of choice empires are often ruined but never founded." He goes on to maintain that no state can be ruined except by the fault of its own citizens. The statesmanship of Philip of Macedon was powerless to overthrow the Athenians; the generalship of Pyrrhus could not destroy the republic of Rome. Where, on the other hand, necessity is disregarded and caprice governs, there are many examples of the fall of empires. This too is overruled by Providence that the barbarians may have their turn. In a marginal note on a later page we read that the beginning of war is free but the result is a matter of necessity.[23] He adds, however, that though states may be founded by violence and fraud, they are maintained by pursuing the ends of humane culture. Necessity, to Vico, is something different from what it is to Machiavelli. It is law and the working of Providence through the needs of human nature. It is almost the categorical imperative in politics. It is further the survival of the best. The sentence just quoted is the germ of a doctrine more fully elaborated in the *Scienza Nuova*.

He had long been pondering the nature of the laws that mould the character of the generations. He had written in 1708 that minds are formed by language and not language by minds.[24] He quotes with approval Caraffa's remark that the characters of men are formed by the institutions under which they live. In the *de Antiquissima*[25] he compares fate to a word, uttered by God, and the successive events are the cases of its declension. In commencing the biography of Caraffa, he traces an evolutionary law even in the history of biography. In early times biographies are written about men of virtue or valour, in accordance with the spirit of primitive ages. Later when social organization is more elaborate, the subjects of biography are selected from men exercising real power in the state. Finally, in the general decline, the lives of those men are written who are merely conspicuous by their position and illustrate in their character the growing demoralization.

Whilst echoing the phrases of Machiavelli and negating his doctrine, Vico reacts positively to Grotius. It was now that he added Grotius to the other three authors, Plato, Tacitus and Bacon, whom he continually studied. He says in the autobiography that his work on Caraffa obliged him to read the *de jure Belli et Pacis*. "Grotius," he writes, "has put into a system of universal right the philosophy and theology . . . both of the history of actual or fabulous events and of the three learned languages of antiquity, Hebrew, Greek and Latin." The reason why Vico felt forced to read International Law in order to write the biography of a general is clear from his inaugural oration of 1705. War, which suspends the ordinary operations of law, throws upon the military commander the responsibilities of equity. The judgment on Grotius just quoted shows that Vico now viewed history as the expression in events of certain fundamental ideas, which ideas were theological and philosophical in character. The individualistic historiography of the Renascence derives from Plutarch and Machiavelli. Modern historiography, taking its orientation from collective humanity, historiography as conceived by Vico, by Comte, by Marx and by Vico's conscious disciple Michelet, derives from Grotius. Vico thought for a time of editing Grotius, but he was deterred by the reflection "that it did not become a man Catholic in religion, to adorn with notes the work of a heretic."

The biography of Caraffa was published in 1716. With the money he received for it Vico was able to pay the dowry of his daughter Luisa, who was married the next year. Another reward of the two years of intense labour was the friendship and esteem of Gravina. The intimate correspondence thus initiated continued for the few months of life that still remained to Gravina. They never met and their letters have not survived. The importance of Gravina's influence on Vico must remain a matter of conjecture. The chief philosophical influence in Gravina's own life had been the Cartesian. He had, though only for a short time, been a pupil of Caloprese; he had been initiated by him into philosophy and ancient learning. In Greek scholarship he was by far Vico's superior. He was a pioneer in the history of Roman law and in the theory of poetry. He had written the best historical account yet known of Roman law of which he had a philosophical conception approaching that which Vico was at the same time studying in Grotius. In this work, the first part of which was published in 1701 under the title, *de Ortu et Progressu Juris Civilis*, he wrote, "Civil law is nothing but natural law applied to the establishment of the Roman state, reason expressed in Roman manners and letters."[26] He did not, however, anticipate the ideas which Vico was to enunciate in 1720. It was Vico who first investigated the evolution, in law and custom, of the mind of the Roman people. Gravina inclined to the views which had hitherto prevailed, that individual founders of states account for their character and destiny, and that the patrician order were the descendants of men selected by Romulus. But a close intercourse with Gravina in the crucial time between the *de Rebus Gestis Antonii Caraphaei* and the *de Uno Universi Juris Principio* cannot fail to have been full of suggestion for Vico. It involves, indirectly, Cartesian influence on Vico. The Cartesian standard and explanation in literature, science, history and philosophy was reason. Poetry ought to be embodied reason. History had been depreciated by Descartes but not by his Neapolitan followers Caloprese, Doria and Gravina. Gravina saw in Roman law embodied reason. He saw, like Vico, the importance of origins and the importance of philology for this study.[27] But it was not given to him to apply this conception so as to yield a philosophy of history. This task was left to the far more original genius of Vico.

Gravina was thoroughly Cartesian in his theory of poetry. He is one of the founders of modern criticism.[28] Three writers of that age in Italy defined the function of the imagination in literary creation, Muratori, Gravina and Vico. But though for Gravina poetry was vision, it was vision in the service of rational and moral teaching. Homer, for him, was a sage who, for the purpose of educating his countrymen, clothed his abstract doctrine with poetical beauty in order to communicate it to the ordinary mind. Here again, as we shall see, Vico's conclusions were very different from and far more profound than Gravina's. One other point of contact must be mentioned. Gravina was one of those who revived the study of Dante in Italy. Vico had many years before recognized Dante as the chief Italian poet.

CHAPTER X

A PHILOSOPHY OF JURISPRUDENCE

In the inaugural oration of 1719 Vico declared that "our present philology is uncertain, obscure, irrational, fabulous and quite incapable of being reduced to scientific principles." He had by this time made great progress towards new conceptions of history. In the next year he published an elaborate treatise on jurisprudence, with special reference to the early laws of Rome. It was entitled *De uno universi juris principio et fine uno*. He put forth about the same time a synopsis not only of this work but also of the rather longer work, *De constantia jurisprudentis*, which was published in 1721. The two books are sometimes combined under the title of *Diritto* (or *Jus*) *Universale*.

With the autobiographer's instinct for noting the occasion of any change in his thinking, and the scholar's tendency to attribute his original thoughts to the stimulus of the printed page, he says that he was one day reading the thirty-first chapter of the fourth book of Augustine's *City of God*, in which is discussed Varro's judgment of Roman religion. Varro declared that, had he been given the task of providing the Romans with a new religion, he would have given them a faith according to Nature, with one incorporeal and infinite Deity in place of their innumerable idols. As if a fresh light had dawned for him, Vico applied Varro's natural religion to Law of Nature in the juristic sense. The true God is the principle or beginning not only of true religion but of true jurisprudence. The search for a metaphysic of law became a passion; "a mighty desire entered my soul." The study of Grotius had helped Vico up to a point. He saw that social institutions must be examined historically and psychologically. But Grotius was wrong, he thought, in saying that they could be explained from human nature alone.

Vico's first attempt to give to the philosophy of human society at once a theological and a psychological orientation was a false start. Finding in man as well as in God the three attributes of knowledge, will and power, he regarded them as enabling human institutions to approximate to the divine law. His application of these divine and human principles of jurisprudence is highly arbitrary. The three attributes of knowledge, will and power correspond respectively to the three virtues of prudence, temperance and courage, which similarly correspond in the legal sphere to property, liberty and wardship. Property, liberty and wardship together compose authority, first in the solitary individual, then in the family, finally in the state. The tripartite enumeration of functions or departments of the state gives us first, under property (*dominium*), all regulation of ownership, the assessment of classes, tribute and all the business of the treasury; then, under civil liberty, rewards and punishments, honours and burdens; finally, under wardship (*tutela*), which becomes in the state *summum imperium*, all laws, magistracies, judiciary, fortifications, arms, garrisons, war and treaties. Civil authority, comprising all three, is political sovereignty, deriving its justification from its embodiment of the finite knowledge, will and power of man striving towards the infinite knowledge, will and power of God

Whatever the philosophical value of this view of the grounds of political obligation, it is clear that its detailed application here to the different branches of human law is arbitrary and unfruitful for any scientific purpose.[29]

In another connection, however, Vico's treatment in this work of the nature of authority is of the utmost importance for his future thought. Authority is related to certitude as reason is related to truth. The distinction between authority and reason corresponds to the distinction between certitude and truth. We have already learned the distinction between certitude and truth in examining the distinction between consciousness and knowledge in Vico's criticism of the Cartesian formula "I think, therefore I am." Truth and knowledge are of the whole, and are only in God. They are the objects of the divine reason. Certitude, consciousness of a belief which we cannot doubt, is all that belongs to man. This certitude depends not on reason but on authority, the authority of our senses or of our informants or of those who have enacted the laws which we receive as determinate or certain.

Here, however, for the sake of an intelligible first statement of the theory, we are making it too simple. Vico's use of these terms is not consistent. He is a poetical thinker. He suggests in his definitions as much as he defines. He has pregnant ambiguities. His use of the word certainty, certitude (*certum*) is one of them. Certitude is, in the first place, a partial knowledge, knowledge of a thing without that knowledge of causes which would make it perfect knowledge and convert the certainty into truth. In this sense authority is part of reason, giving us that certitude which it would require reason to complete into truth. Secondly, whereas truth is always in agreement with the objective or real order of things, certitude is subjective, its validity for us consisting in our mere inability to doubt. In the third place, certitude is empirical, a state of mind dependent on experience or tradition (authority) and not on reason. Authority, the parent of certitude, is in general the region of the human will, and so of history and politics. But progress in these fields consists in the gradual assimilation of authority to reason which is the sphere of divine order and truth. The understanding of Vico's whole teaching about history, to the end of his life, depends on a grasp of these conceptions and their mutual relations.

Authority is a term of similar pregnancy. The doctrine of truth and the doctrine of right are closely connected in Vico. We have seen that in him the good and the true are one in the divine, creative mind. Authority is the source of the right, the true and the achieved, the realized or made in the lower sphere of certitude, as reason is in the higher sphere of truth. Before families were, there was authority in the solitary individual to maintain his being in knowledge, will and power. This authority was the sum both of his rights and of his history. The authority of the family and finally of the state is the historical continuation and successor to this authority, guaranteeing and limiting it at the same time. Authority is experience, tradition, law and right, the whole story of will in its progress towards reason; of humanity in its return to God, from whom it originated.

The distinction between cause and occasion, explained by Vico ten years earlier in his metaphysical book, retains its importance here. Writers like Machiavelli and Hobbes, who regarded human necessities and desires as the causes of events and progress, are attributing to man what pertains to God, who is not merely the first but the only cause. By so doing they remove history from the sphere of ethics and religion, and make justice subordinate to expediency. One event is the occasion, not the cause, of another. Causality being in God, the good alone is the cause of the actual. Justice therefore consists in a right relation between cause (*honestas* or the good) and occasion (*utile* or opportune). Where the utilities of life, such things as the Stoics regarded as neither good nor evil in themselves but indifferent, are distributed in accordance with reason, there the laws are just. The expression of this justice when fully realized is *equum bonum*, equal distribution of utilities. "What in regard to choice is just, in regard to measure is equal." But between the state and the private citizen or between the head and members of a family the just principle is one of inequality. This forms the most important difference between public and private law.[30]

Such is Vico's philosophical approach to history. He was convinced that the history of institutions could only be written in the light of a true philosophy. In this philosophy they must find their origin and their principle of development. The explanation of history was partly prehistoric and partly metaphysical. History, he says, had been misunderstood for want of its beginnings, and a knowledge of these could only be supplied by philosophy. But it was not only the beginnings that philosophy must supply. The true nature of historical causation must also be found. So long as human occasions were taken as causes, and until it was realized that causation was only in God, the truth of history as an account of the work of Providence would never be seen.

The condition of mankind in its progressive task of rationalizing its institutions, of making authority conform gradually to truth and reason, is *humanitas*. Mankind is assumed to start from a condition in which it is devoid of humanity. The Christian Vico evades the garden of Eden by assuming that after the great deluge men were scattered "through the great forest of the world" in search of food and in flight from beasts until they were themselves reduced to brutish isolation and simplicity. He supposes that they lose even the use of language. There is no regulation of lust or violence and, in fact, no society.

The first task of philosophy as applied to history is to discover how men emerged from this condition, how "humanity" began. Clearly the current theory that political society began with a contract is of no use here. The recognition of a social bond necessarily precedes contract. The problem has become that of the origin of conscience, the sense of obligation on which the keeping of any contract will depend. Vico sometimes defines *humanitas* as the disposition of man to help man. His theory is that conscience and religion originate in fear. He imagines brutish men startled in the act of canine or shameless copulation with captured women by thunder from the sky. This is the origin of shame, *pudor*, which resulted from these men being terrified into the secrecy of caves or deep woods for their sexual intercourse. These caves become the centres of the first families, which make the first division of lands. Settled or localized habitation leads to the burial of the dead. From the word *humare*, to bury, Vico derives the word *humanitas*.[31]

The origin of the state is found, not, as had been customary since the time of Aristotle, in a mere agglomeration of these families, but in groupings of families of a different and later kind. The first cave-dwellers, educating their wives and children in the religion of the sky, the thundering Jove, live surrounded by the wilderness where still rove the brutish, unhumanized beings into whom no opportune thunder-storm has flashed the spark of salutary terror. Here the weak are the prey of the strong. The time comes when fugitives ask protection from the settled families. Their violent pursuers prove no match for men strengthened by continence and co-operation, and are slain at the borders of the fields; the boundary-stones become the first altars besprent with blood. The heroic age has now dawned, the heads and warriors of the settled families being the heroes. By the reception of the fugitives the nature of the family is changed. It has become a clan whose members are of two degrees. The heroes and their wives and children are the nucleus. The hero unites in himself all authority. He is the priest, the chieftain and the wise man. He is the law-giver and his marriage has the sanction of religion. It is he who practices divination, the art of consulting the sky where the divine power resides. The other grade of people in this enlarged family are the fugitives, who have been received into a condition resembling serfdom, without legal rights, without religious marriage, without property. They were obliged to respect the religion of the sky, but they had no part in its privileges and its wisdom. They could not take the auspices or practise divination. Still they were part of the larger family and in return for protection they cultivated the lands of their masters.

Only as arising from families with dependents of this kind, Vico thinks, can the first forms of political life of which early history shows traces receive a credible explanation. History for him means primarily the history of Rome. There he finds the fullest representation of the different stages through which society has passed. His theory of origins gives a far more satisfactory account of the origins of the patrician and plebeian orders than the derivation of the patricians from the choice of individuals by Romulus. He does not confine himself to Roman history. He draws evidence from Greece or from any account of remoter peoples given by travellers ancient or modern. His common proceeding was to brood patiently over the laws and history of ancient Rome by the light of as much of his theory as he had already formulated and to accept as corroborative any helpful detail from the history of other lands. His nomenclature he takes from Rome. After describing the condition of the fugitives in the community of heroes, he says that the histories of Spain, Africa and other countries "overflow with clients," or semi-servile dependents.[32]

What follows bears out his contention that history can only be understood through its origins, through pre-history, which he claims to have supplied by his philosophy. No contract can explain the first state. Kingship comes into being when the plebeians, weary of cultivating the land for nothing, begin to claim rights. Against their combination the heroes band themselves together under a leader who becomes the first king. Not that the first form of government is monarchic as had generally been assumed. The king is essentially the head of an aristocracy. The first concessions made to the plebeians are the first agrarian laws. Vico sees in the contest between the orders the staple thread of Roman history, indeed of any history that is true to type. The course of this contest can only be understood when we understand the primitive religion, the heroes and the fugitives. Then only do we see why and how the struggle was for improved conditions of land-tenure, for the right of intermarriage, for legality of status, for the publication of the laws which had been the secret tradition of the patricians, and for the right to hold office; also why and how this right was connected with divination and auspices.

In the long unfolding of legal changes in the history of Rome the patricians represent authority and the plebeians represent reason. Authority is in the letter of the law which is at first rigid.[33] The approximation of law to equity, the gradual establishment of equal rights, comes about through the efforts of the plebeians to acquire full *humanitas*. This vindication of the rational nature of man as such is a historical process. It is the work of Providence in two senses. The goal is set by Providence, being the return of man to the divine nature; and the means are ordained by Providence which has made man with social needs and has placed him in circumstances which render their satisfaction a progressive realization of justice.[34]

Vico was far in advance of any of his contemporaries in his understanding that every stage of social progress is an organic whole, that language, art, polity and religion all interpenetrate one another so that a special stage of any one of them belongs to certain special stages of the others. The main divisions of the story of *humanitas* are more clearly marked in his later works. He tends

already, however, to speak of them as three, the first
being theocratic, the second heroic and the third political.
He believed the historic cycle recurred. He grasped the
fact that the conditions of the Homeric world were as
feudal as those of the middle ages of Christendom. He
sees the same feudal character in the relation between a
Roman patrician and his clients. The feudal relation
arises in the "heroic" period but survives far into the
political period. Another survival which is built into and
ultimately superseded by the political structure is the
authority of the head of the family, whose right of private
violence is gradually merged into the right of public
violence, the punitive function of the state. In his view of
this function he is highly original. Dividing crimes into
those of ignorance, those of weakness or incontinence and
those of brutishness or want of the common sense of
humanity, he considers criminals of the first class as
adequately punished by the shame or remorse of coming to
a knowledge of their guilt, whilst the aim of punishment in
the case of the incontinent is reformation. The third class
cannot be reformed; there punishment is to be exemplary
or deterrent. The introduction of conscience or shame for
wrong-doing into a treatise of jurisprudence has been
criticized as a confusion of morality and law. But in Vico
it goes back to the origins of civil society, because shame
and conscience, occasioned first by superstitious fear,
are the original sanctions of all obligation.

CHAPTER XI

PHILOSOPHY AND PHILOLOGY

IN the treatise thus terminated, its author had only given half his new thoughts to the world, had only developed his historical theories from one point of view, that of jurisprudence. The work itself shows that it was only a part of a larger body of doctrine. Taken by itself it seems to lack symmetry, to be without the elucidations in the fields of history and philology which are necessary to its completeness. There are times when it seems to be the sketch of a new view of general history, others when the subject of jurisprudence is treated from a purely philosophical standpoint. It is well to remember that the first readers of the work were without that knowledge of Vico's complete system which most modern readers possess by having first read his later works. It was clear to all that he possessed great learning and ingenuity. But his proofs must have appeared inadequate, far fetched and fantastic. Arbitrary deductions thrust their tentacles through a web woven of profound historical perceptions, ingenious or naïve etymologies, controverted theological doctrines and the beginnings of a systematic social psychology, whilst the main stream along which we are carried is the constitutional history of Rome treated as the normal development of a typical state. At the same time it is obvious, from his own account, that the development thus regarded as normal was shared by the state taken as typical with no other state in the history of the world, whilst only a few Greek states approximated to it in some degree. The vision of a comparative history of institutions appears at moments and vanishes almost immediately. A specious unity of metaphysics and history dissolves on the first serious analysis. It must have been difficult for men of either the scholastic or the Cartesian way of thinking to detect what was new and valuable in such a work, to realize that behind all this strange exposition was a mind thinking in terms of sciences yet unborn. Vico himself afterwards regarded the works of these years as completely superseded by what he wrote later. But we can now see that he already conceived the relation of historical events to the mind of man in ways of which only much later thinkers have understood the true significance, and which some important thinkers since his time have for the most part failed to perceive. The man who wrote the treatise of 1720 would never, for example, have derived events directly from economic conditions without interposing psychology. Nor would he have missed, as, for example, so brilliant a historian as Voltaire missed, the interdependence and relative importance of different periods of history. There is already in Vico, in 1720, if not a philosophy of history, at least the beginning of a morphology of human culture.

(1) *Truth and Speech*

The second part of the *Diritto Universale* was published in 1721 under the title of *de Constantia Jurisprudentis Liber Alter*, and itself consisted of two parts, *de Constantia Philosophiae* and *de Constantia Philologiae*. The former lays down in a very few pages the theological and philosophical foundations of the latter. In it we read that true religion has appeared on earth in two forms, first as the religion of Adam in his first state of intercourse with God; Adam was then above the need of laws. The second form of true religion is Christianity with Judaism as prologue. Vico's task is with the false religions, to explain the evolution of the secular world. Even in these false religions there is the seed of truth. Though pagan virtue attains only to the control of selfish passion and not to its surrender to divine grace as in Christian humility, the development of the pagan nations from violence, authority and tradition to reason and equity is a real ascent under the guidance of Providence. The pagan philosophers had some knowledge of truth, especially Plato with his understanding that temporal things depend upon the things that are eternal.

God, for Vico, is pure mind. In so far as the life of will and sense in man comes to be ordered by reason, the human world comes to resemble the divine reality which alone truly is. But at every stage the seeds of truth are present in humanity, and evil is only the absence of good, since God is the cause of all that exists. The end is therefore continually realized, not merely attained at the conclusion of the process.

The first chapter of the work *de Constantia Philologiae* is headed *Nova scientia tentatur*, and caused, thinks Vico, some annoyance to the critics, with its ambitious title which to us is so full of significance. The new philological science is a part of philosophy since authority is a part of reason. Since words represent ideas or things, philology embraces the whole history of articulate man, the manners, traditions, laws, politics and disciplines of tribes and peoples. It ascribes words and all they signify to the ages to which historically they belong, and explains all their mutations and successions. Such a science did not yet exist. The obscure shapes of historical characters no more appeared to scholars in their true proportions, relations and distances than did the constellations as they were imagined before Copernicus. To reveal the human past and the laws of social development, to ascertain that such laws there were, and that Providence was not, as represented by Bossuet, handling puppets, was a task which, in its interest and importance, might well be ranked with the discovery that unveiled the heavens.

In the work of 1720 the development of the human mind and of society had been sketched from the point of view of the history of law. In 1721, after some preliminary chapters for the benefit of critics of the earlier book, the whole historic process is treated from the point of view of the history of language. The chief problem in this investigation is the nature of the speech of early man. With his conception of history as an unfolding of the seeds of truth and reason from their crudest and most obscure manifestations, Vico necessarily believed the earliest language to be that of rude and simple men, living more by the senses and the imagination than by reason. He was therefore able to study the nature of early man in children and savages.

(2) *The Invention of Poetry*

In the answers Vico was now finding to his questions, he leads us far into unexplored land, justifying amply the title of that ambitious first chapter. His solution of the problem of primitive speech lay in the discovery that it was essentially poetical. Children and savages are incapable of much abstract thinking, their mental representations are concrete; and poetry presents its objects preferably in concrete form. Their predominant faculty is imagination; this is also the faculty exercised in poetry. According to tradition poetry was written before prose; it may therefore have been spoken before prose. Early, brutish men, according to Vico, had lost the use of speech through their scattering after the great deluge. The problem therefore assumes the form of accounting for the invention of language; and, early language being poetical, what has to be discovered is the way in which those forms of language were invented that are specially poetical.

On the nature of poetry a flood of books had been poured out in Italy since the Renascence, and the highly artificial and self-conscious literature of the baroque period had stimulated aesthetic theorizing. Homer, Virgil, Ariosto, Tasso had been championed, denounced, compared and set over against one another as battle-flags of controversy. Learned war had been waged between the French and Italians. Whole books had been written on the difference between acuteness and arguteness. But practically the whole of this literature had been logical, formal, abstract and analytical. Vico was not so much interested in how Aristotle or any other critic had defined this or that form of poetry, this or that figure of speech.[35] The questions he asked himself were how men, such as he conceived them long ago to have lived and felt, could or rather must have invented these forms of language, and what history of mankind a study of language would reveal.

It was, therefore, a question of invention; the faculty of invention he called *ingenium*. Early men having the mentality of boys, the question of how invention occurred in the childhood of the race can be answered from the study of boys endowed with *ingenium*, "ingenious boys." Vico had the strange belief that when children wish to name anything, they run through their whole vocabulary to find the proper word. It does not seem to have occurred to him that the word is recalled by its object, that the two are directly associated, that the child with a new thing to be named thinks at once of some object already named which it resembles, and the name comes. The law of mental association was only beginning to be understood. Hobbes and Spinoza had appreciated it more fully than did Vico, who, though a profound psychologist, fails to see the application of this law to names and the things they denominate.

Vico supposes that men who had lost the habit of speech, perhaps for generations, would, from long disuse of the physical organs, find difficulty in articulation. The first words would be little more than exclamatory, mono-syllabic noises, and they would be few. The development of language involved the extended use of a comparatively small number of expressions to signify new objects of perception, new institutions and new thoughts. This extension was affected by what later came to be called figures of speech. In a poverty of words the necessity of new uses became the mother of invention, not so often the invention of new words as of devices for making the old word serve a new purpose. There being no word to express drought, the land was said to thirst. Thus *metaphor* was born. Two principles determine its creation. The new phenomenon will be named from something that resembles it; and this principle of similarity will be modi-

fied by the tendency to use expressions already representing the things that have most powerfully affected the
senses. By *synechdoche* the most common or noticeable
species gives its name to the whole genus, every large
bird being called an eagle and every small one a sparrow.
The *pleonasms* and conventional adjectives of which Homer
is full are due to the tendency, obvious in children and
barbarians, to rely on attributes from an inability to
comprehend substance. Perhaps the most important
figure of speech for Vico is *autonomasia*, the giving of the
same name to a number of individuals having like
qualities, so that every hero becomes Hercules. This
becomes the key to Vico's reform of chronology and
mythology. The figure known as *hypotyposis*, or vivid
picturing, a kind of metaphor, corresponds to the com-
parisons and circumlocutions to which "ingenious boys"
are often driven by their want of words or of ideas.
Unable to conceive the zodiacal period of a year, they will
speak of the number of harvests that have passed. Unable
to grasp so abstract a notion as "for ever," they will say
"so long as the rivers flow into the sea." But above all,
they will have recourse to *onomatopoeia*. Vico quotes the
Homeric *siz'* (our "sizzle"), and Dante's *cric* for the
sound of breaking ice. And then these boys, when they
don't know a word, will simply leave it out. By this last
means the language of early men gained that elliptical
and compressed character which is so effective in poetry.
And, since their senses are acute and their emotions very
strong, they will exaggerate. Vico in his walks reflected
that the steep mountains of his boyhood, when he was
doubtless as "ingenious" as any, had sunk to insignificant
slopes to the accurate eye of manhood. Hence Roland's

incredible blast; hence gods of more than human stature. The poet's strong turn for pathetic forms of speech and for the sublime is likewise to be found in children and, Vico adds, in women. Thus Sappho, in the ode which Catullus translated: *Ille mihi par esse deo videtur*; every astonishing man is equalled with a god. This chapter fully bears out the claim made for Vico of being a close observer of children and rustics. He was not only an observer; he went far towards creating a psychology of childhood.[36]

All these tropes, exaggerations, sublimities, personifications and fables of the poets depend for their origin upon genuine ignorance and simplicity, and on the fact that imagination had to do the work later done by reason. Their invention required the spur of overwhelming necessity. So far as they had progressed in an age of ignorance they were available for later poets who used them with professed artifice. The truth of science has destroyed the conditions that favour great poetry. Vico propounds a new art of poetry. Whoever would be a poet must forget the wealth of words that enables him to describe an event as it actually happened. He must confine himself to language that is sensuous and impassioned, and find out the means of saying in such language all that he has to say, as primitive men were forced to do. He must disown the scientific and philosophical approach to life, must learn to think and feel as boys and rustics think and feel, and must know what tropes and pictures will reduce modern readers to a corresponding degree of credulity. He will work with as much art as a rhetorician, giving the lie to the maxim that poets are born and orators are made. He must work, above all, with his imagination, must become a supreme phantast.[37]

Another characteristic of poetry, its rhythm, must be otherwise accounted for than as a pleasing device of civilized poets; clearly it preceded all civilization. It was not because, in the absence of writing, rhythmical sayings were the easiest to remember, that poetical rhythm was invented. It was for Vico not art but nature. It was not literature and the occasional speech of the few but the only speech of all men when they first attained to speech. It arose not from wealth of means but from limitation, under conditions not of sophistication but of crudity. Vico had noticed, what is known to educationists to-day, that stammerers can overcome their impediment by breaking into song. When men first attained to speech after the brutish solitude and dumbness of their dispersion, their vocal organs were stiff and clumsy. They had to help themselves to utterance with spurts of rhythmic excitation.

In some notes written soon afterwards Vico gave a remarkable instance of rudimentary thinking in Homer, who wrote, as if men's minds were something apart from them and unknown to them, "the sacred strength of Antinous understood," and "the sacred force of Telemachus spoke." Here the chief characteristic of the hero, his strength, is used to denominate his mind, a something, however, separate from his common, visible self. "And the plural minds is used for mind, spirits for spirit, as if each thought were a separate mind, and every act of volition a fresh will or spirit." This failure to generalize is remarked by Sir Henry Maine in *Ancient Law*, where he points out that each legal decision was a separate Themis or personified Justice coming to the judge. It is extraordinary to find it remarked by Vico in the infancy of modern psychology.[38] But it is a case in which the intuition of genius owed its sureness, not to an isolated flash of insight, but to the organic wholeness and unity of a mind capable of creating a "new science."

The investigation into the origin of poetry leads to a revolution in the conception of its nature. It had almost always been assumed either that poetry had a didactic purpose, or else that it was a luxury. The two theories were combined in the assumption that poets wrote practical wisdom or philosophical truth for readers who could not or would not attend to abstruse reasoning. Some writers emphasize the importance of imagination. But to Vico imagination meant vastly more than the faculty of reducing precepts to picturesque form. For him the whole mind of early man was imagination and conceived the whole of experience and reflection imaginatively. In the synopsis of 1720 the necessary character of this early poetry is stated in a very clear argument. Man is forced by the nature of things to secure first what is necessary; the first philosophers contemplated the physical universe. After the necessary men can attend to the convenient or becoming, and moral questions receive attention; this phase is marked by the teaching of Socrates. Finally, there is leisure to seek what is pleasing, or else, with Plato, to pursue philosophy into the heights. Poetry, because it is the earliest form of utterance, belongs to the category of what is necessary. It is prior historically to the merely convenient or ornamental. It was early man's only way of speaking of the highest things. "Nature not art" is the phrase that sums up Vico's theory of poetry— one of the great, rough-hewn monuments of the history of thought.

(3) *The Ages of Man*

In a chronological table prefixed to this work, based on the current beliefs of his age which fixed the Deluge in the year of the world 1656, Vico divides all time into three periods, the obscure, the fabulous and the historical. The obscure period ends when Grecian chronology begins, with the establishment of Olympian games by Hercules. It is partly filled with events recorded in the Old Testament or by very ancient tradition; but there are long spaces of empty, unrecorded time. The fabulous period is rich in fable and has to be understood through the interpretation of fables. The true interpretation has been lost because of the change in human mentality. It is Vico's purpose to recover it. The historical period begins with the second Punic war, from which "Livy professes to be able to write a true history of Rome." In the obscure period are two distinct stages of "humanity." We have seen the origin of human culture in religion, a religion connected with the sky and giving rise to divination and a primitive theology. This religion rules the "divine" period, when human wisdom found utterance in the language of the "theological poets." Vico had a very subtle sense of the complex influences by which one phase of society gives place to another. We should search in vain for a clear line between periods. In a short work like the present it is quite impossible to convey that feeling of immense respect for his imaginative realization of the character of change in human affairs which grows upon the careful reader of his volumes. Nowhere more than in him do we feel the truth of the maxim that all times are transitional. His master might, indeed, have been Hera-

clitus, for he has two things, above all, to teach. The one
is that each period differs from its successor. The other
is that the past is to be understood by its survivals, by its
influence on the present, by the chain of causality which
is the element of consistency in the perpetual flow of life.
When he says "the first heroes founded cities not for
themselves and their followers but for the gods," he shows
the theocratic age extending its influence into the heroic
age and political institutions in the germ at the beginning
of the age of heroes.39 The heroic age starts before the
end of the obscure time, occupies the whole of the
fabulous time and continues after the foundation of
states. But before the clear historic era has opened, the
heroic elements are giving way to modes of life and
forms of polity based in large measure upon the rational
doctrine of equal justice.

The first period of humanized mankind is "divine"
in the supposed reception of all its knowledge and
authority directly from the gods, and above all in the
theological character of its language. Its science was
"divination." The powers of nature, and still more such
of the large simple realities of society as a primitive people
could express in language, were indicated by the names
of the twelve greater and older gods of Greco-Roman
mythology, the *dii majorum gentium*, that is, the gods of
the time before the foundation of cities. The poets were
then "theological." Before the invention of the heroic
language there was a "divine" language. This had been
called in question, but Homer bears witness to it, and
speaks of things that had one name in the language of
the gods, another in that of men. Homer himself no
doubt supposed that he was merely telling us how the

gods called a thing by one name and men by another. But in Homer's time the "divine" language had been forgotten. Vico, knowing that the false gods never existed, sees that the duplicate nomenclature meant more than Homer could guess. His "language of the gods" is the "divine" language, the language of men in a pre-Homeric period of theological poets. "To the first men all things were divine." They use the word, accordingly, with great freedom, and write of "divine strength," the "divine sea," and even the "divine swineherd" of Ulysses, all examples of the survival and therefore proofs of the former existence of the "divine" language. Vico cannot resist the opportunity to gibe at the pantheism of some of the modern deists. By making everything divine they showed themselves very primitive in their philosophy.[40]

Whilst in the language of the earliest period everything was referred to the gods, whose names, or characters, were the fundamental vehicle of expression, the subject-matter conveyed in that language is seen by Vico likewise to have been something other than it had generally been supposed. It is one of his most revolutionary propositions that mythology is not to be interpreted as of the physical universe but as of human society. The theological poets were the ancestors not of natural but of political philo-sophers. Chaos is not the primal confusion of the physical elements, but the utter confusion of human stocks in the great dispersion after the flood, the confusion out of which first families and clans, and then states, gradually took form. Jupiter is certainly at first almost identified with the sky, but his original manifestation, when he scared the brutish men into pudicity, was a fact of social significance. And by a figure of speech, like that of "ingenious boys" who, wanting for words, call all men "father," or rather "tata," the theologico-political poets called all the gods father, that being the sole term of authority in the primitive age of families. Hence the forms, Diëspiter, Marspitor, and the title of *mater* given to Juno and Venus. The name Zeus is onomatopoeic, resembling the hissing of the thunderbolt. Jove's eagle is the bird of the sky, that is of divination, and to say that the sceptre had an eagle on it was to attribute rights of divination to the king, or earlier, the father, who had the sceptre. The sceptre itself with the eagle on it was a mute language expressing all this without words. Indeed, going further back, Vico declared that the first language was a language of mute signs, thus identifying in their origins speech and writing, which at first was a hieroglyphic or divine language of pictures. The phonetic alphabet he regarded as subsequent to an elementary knowledge of mathematics; but also as onomatopoeic, the roundest vowel O representing the roundest sound, the thinnest sound being represented by I. Vico sees that the use of the phonetic alphabet was a great advance and involved higher and more difficult mental operations.

The myth is an expanded metaphorical sentence. When the early poet-men spoke of Pegasus, the winged horse, they meant that the fathers, or heroes, those who had the right of divination indicated by wings, invented the art of riding on horseback. Mercury, Saturn and Amor are all given wings, and all represent different facts about the patrician order, or rather its ancestors the heroes. They recognize in their worship of the winged Mercury their own function of conserving and interpreting the laws which are given from heaven to those that have the right of auspices, an exclusive right long guarded by the patricians. Wings on the god of love mean that only the heroes, the *patres*, have the true and sacred form of marriage. Saturn has wings, but not because time flies. That is a false interpretation by the later and artificial poets. Saturn is the god of harvests and cultivation. The heroes, signified by wings, as having the exclusive right of divination, invented cultivation. Therefore the early men attached wings to Saturn as we now join a predicate to a subject. The junction of two symbols was to them what the junction of two words by a copula is to us. By the time of Homer, who lived late in the heroic age, the significance of the very symbols and myths which gave sublimity to his poems was to a great extent lost. In fact by his time the heroic age was in a state of decline morally, and gave lascivious interpretation to ancient myths which had originally possessed far other and more innocent meanings. An example of this is the story of Juno's jealousy and punishment, and her persecution of Hercules. The poets by Homer's time had woven a decadent romance about it. But originally Hercules was not an individual in a romance. By a principle of the poetic early language which, as we have seen, gave the name of Hercules to every man who possessed his qualities, he was the heroic age itself, and his labours were the achievements of the heroes, their invention of tillage and of the other arts fundamental to civilization. Juno sets these tasks because she is the goddess of legitimate marriage and therefore from one point of view presides over the heroic period. Hercules is the son of Jupiter as the primary father-god of the fathers, or heroes, and of Venus who represents human beauty. Juno is suspended from heaven with her hands bound by a silver chain because the air signifies divination and divination is both the prelude to the legitimate marriage of the heroes and their special function and privilege. The heavy anvils attached to her feet signify the firm and indissoluble character of such matrimony. In forming this concatenation of symbolical objects the primitive poets were simply putting together into an intelligible sequence what to them were the equivalents of words; they were making sentences. They were not composing fictitious narratives but stating facts of law, religion and social organization. Another example of current misinterpretation is the idea of an age of gold. The original gold was corn. The name was afterwards given to the metal metonymically because it had the colour of corn. The age of gold is therefore the age of agriculture. The golden bough, to which, if it were plucked, another succeeded, meant the harvest, on which, after it was reaped, another followed; whilst the descent of Aeneas into Hell, means the sowing of corn, or the invention of agriculture. Hercules, Aeneas, Theseus, Romulus are the heroes, or rather the heroic age itself and all its achievements. This explains their appearance over a series of years far longer than a single lifetime. So the anachronisms in the fables become, not a reason for rejecting, but a means of interpreting them.[41]

Such are the principles, and many more examples might have been given, upon which Vico reconstructs the history of the obscure age, which he divides into five periods. In the first all government is theocratic, and the solitary men begin to form families. In the second the families are augmented by clients, whose importance for the formation of political society had been explained in the book on jurisprudence. In the third emerge the kingdoms, the heroic kingdoms of the optimates or patricians. In the fourth these aristocracies give place either to monarchies or to free republics. In the fifth is introduced the *jus minorum gentium*, which is the law of the state superseding the laws of the patricians. This division joins into one the obscure and fabulous ages; Vico says, in fact, that the obscure and fabulous ages are seen to be one, which seems to mean that he interprets their records by the same principles of research. That which in Vico is far in advance of his time is the way in which the stage of mental development determines for each successive period the character of every manifestation of human thought;—religion, science, manners, laws, states, judicial proceedings, wars and commerce.

The whole historic cycle ends in God. This affirmation has two meanings. The first is that, whereas human beings are now organized in states under government, the states are under no common ruler but God. The theocracy has therefore returned. The second meaning is that, as the state develops, its internal affairs are ordered more and more in accordance with the laws of equal justice and the rational mind of God. It was this evolution that fitted the Roman Empire to embrace the Christian religion and enabled Justinian to preface his laws with an invocation of the Trinity.

CHAPTER XII

LIFE AND WORK (1720–1725)

THE five or six years ending in 1725 were for Vico years of anxiety, disappointment and intense creative activity. Around him the storm of religious intolerance was again raging, and it struck more than one of his eminent fellow citizens. Giannone's *Civil History of Naples* was the first modern masterpiece of constitutional history, but it was also a learned polemic against the claims of the papacy. The clergy raised a popular tumult against the courageous author and he was hounded from the city, to be treacherously inveigled on to the territory of Savoy and there imprisoned for ten years. A less tragic adventure befel the prominent magistrate Grimaldi. His offence was to have asserted the orthodoxy of Gassendi, Descartes and Malebranche. Failing to obtain permission to print, he had the printing done in his own house. The cardinal-viceroy ordered his almoner to throw the edition into the bay of Naples, with the maledictions prescribed for such cases. "More stones and fewer curses," murmured the boatman as the volumes refused to sink. Some of the copies, washed ashore, were kept as curiosities by their finders. Years later, after a long process at Rome and a change of popes, Grimaldi obtained a lifting of the ban.

Vico, who in early life had been associated with free-thinking and anti-papal authors, appears to have had nothing to do with Giannone, though their lives run closely parallel in the same city. They must frequently have seen one another in Valletta's library. Giannone was a favourite pupil of d'Aulisio, Vico's colleague and close friend. In all his writings Vico never mentions Giannone or his work; nor does he seem to have had anything to do with Grimaldi. The shadow of these clouds of intolerance is very distinct in his correspondence. His reputation had clearly once been blown upon and critics were reviving the scandal. We do not know who his enemies were. He writes sometimes as if each of his publications was met by a storm of malevolent abuse and he is peculiarly sensitive to attack on grounds of theology. Among the literary acquaintance with whom he carried on a petty traffic in mutual adulation, monks and preachers were cultivated with special assiduity. To Father Giacchi of the Capuchins he writes in July 1720:—

"I am a citizen, and a wide social intercourse is inseparable from my position. Weaknesses and errors from my earliest youth are kept in remembrance." The attacks are "tinged with a simulated piety." The praise and friendship of "a Father Giacchi, the leading light of a religious order pre-eminent in severity and holy living," is a favour from heaven. The writer has been attacked through religion, but religion has become his shield.

Among the works which Vico sent to Giacchi in 1721 was the singular poem entitled *Giunone in Dansa*. In form it is an epithalamium for the marriage of one of the Rocca family. In substance it is a compressed version of the mythology of the *Jus Universale*. To those who had not read the prose works the ode must have been unintelligible. Why should Juno, inviting the gods and goddesses to the nuptial dance, address Venus as "beauty fostering civil offices?" Why did the invitation to Jupiter include his eagle "as the faithful interpreter of his language?" What did the noble bridegroom, Don Giovanni Battista Filomarino, Prince of Rocca, make of it? Perhaps, though it takes thirty-four pages in the latest edition, he read it, since probably he paid for it. Its author takes at the same time the opportunity of praising a number of contemporary authors, some of whom, like Metastasio, were deserving. Giacchi sent a most courteous acknowledgment. He had been afraid of finding, under such a festive title, passages hardly befitting his profession; he finds the Muses on closer acquaintance all very learned and modest.

Soon afterwards encouragement came from abroad. The Genevan Jean Leclerc, having been deprived of his pastorate at Amsterdam on account of his opinions, had become one of the most consistent champions of the freedom of opinion in general. The *Bibliothèque Ancienne et Moderne*, which continued from 1714 to 1727, but was not his first venture of the kind, was a review of the intellectual productions of Europe. He is one of those characters, so important in the history of thought, who, without creating anything themselves for posterity, carry on with efficiency and devotion the intellectual business of their own time and are felt to be rather institutions than individuals. He read his presentation copy of the *de Uno*, and wrote to Vico that his former belief in the inferiority of Italian writers was overthrown by it. Vico says in the autobiography that those who thought well of his book were much encouraged, whilst those of a contrary opinion were equally displeased.

He was soon to be badly in need of encouragement himself. His chair of rhetoric, though his tenure was now permanent, was one of the most poorly endowed. It was not of great dignity and existed chiefly to afford linguistic preparation for the higher courses of instruction. It was pedagogical rather than academic. In 1723 several of the more important quadrennial chairs were vacant, and he decided to contest that of Civil Law.

It is a little difficult for later generations, who know Vico as the greatest Italian of his age, to realize that in this public competition he was expected, by his own account, to waste the hour allotted for the exposition of a set theme, in self-laudation and the explanation of his recent writings. Quite in the style in which he records the scholastic triumphs of his childhood, he now tells how he disappointed his ill-wishers and elicited applause from his judges, at whose head sat the venerable royal chaplain Vidania, who had presided when he won the chair of rhetoric. Even in supplying a failure of memory Vico claims to have shown his great erudition. Yet the decision was against him, and both the autobiography and the correspondence reveal his deep disappointment. He had not, after all, given quite what was expected of a candidate, nor had he created so favourable an impression as he supposed. A recent writer believes that his lecture was too philosophical to satisfy the prevailing school of jurisprudence, whose method he had rejected even as a student. He did not receive a single vote, perhaps because, learning that he had failed and on the advice of his friends, he withdrew his candidature before the votes were cast.[42]

He now gave up all hope of gaining any position of

importance in his native city. He was admitted to be one of the best teachers in the university. An official report had mentioned him as one of the few who drew large audiences. Though a strange figure to many, if we are to credit an anecdote that some thought him mad, his intimate friends were such as d'Aulisio and Doria. But he had remained in a minor academic position for a quarter of a century and was to remain there for the rest of his life. He must go on eking out his little salary by writing complimentary verses for members of the aristocracy, by correcting the compositions of others and by giving private tuition. For him was certainly fulfilled the prayer of the German philosopher who asked to be saved from small victories, and before long, having achieved a victory of quite another order which his contemporaries could not recognize, he was to express, in spite of poverty, his thankfulness that the university had refused him promotion and had left him the leisure for his great work.

Meanwhile it was a little solace to get a second letter from Leclerc, who had now published in Amsterdam very favourable reviews of the *de Uno* and the *de Constantia Jurisprudentis*. These reviews Vico gives translated in his autobiography. They do not show that he was understood by the foreign critic. They consist of summaries from which the world would gather that a learned professor in Naples had written one more book reconciling Christianity with certain aspects of Platonism and condemning scepticism ancient and modern; that he had perceived discrepancies in ancient chronology, as others had begun to do; that he had mixed philosophy, history and etymology in a manner difficult to explain,

and that the books he wrote were, in general, very difficult to read. In spite of the praise with which the summary
was introduced, it is not likely that Leclerc's reviews
induced many persons to read Vico, or gave rise in anyone's mind to the suspicion that new ideas of great
importance were here coming to birth.

Vico's reply shows painfully his thirst and gratitude
for appreciation and his anxiety to be supported. He
thanks Leclerc for conferring on him everlasting fame
and for exposing the stupidity of his detractors, who
thought so highly of themselves. He classifies his oppo-
nents as uncritical pedants who could not bear anyone
to touch the edifice of classical learning as they had
received it, philosophers with certain ready-made tests
of truth who despised learning, and lastly those who,
having neither philosophy nor philology, regarded him
as a senseless innovator and took refuge in the charge
of obscurity. With this letter he sent the Homeric notes
and the canons of mythology which he had written to
supplement his philological book. He sent the packet
by a Dutch sea-captain who had touched at Naples, but
he never heard if it reached his friend in Amsterdam.
Meanwhile admirers occur here and there. A professor
of metaphysics in Padua, Nicola Concina, was writing
to his brother Daniele Concina asking him to buy for
him "all the books of Signor Vico, one of the greatest
and most profound intellects in Europe, stocked with
the most recondite learning." But he, too, finds him
difficult, and would like to come to Naples for a few
years as his pupil. Metastasio praises Vico in a letter to
a friend in Turin. But he gives no evidence of deep
insight. He admired the style and, like everybody else

the learning, and remarked on the author's ambition to explain everything by a principle of his own.

Severe as had been the stroke of adverse fortune which closed all prospect of alleviation in the life of strenuous poverty, and deep as the traces of it are in the scanty evidences of his mood in these years, he lost none of his power of resistance and wasted no time in lethargy. He was now at the summit of creative energy. The profound ideas with which he was working continued to agitate his mind, altering the perspectives of history and compelling ever fresh applications in many paths of thought. The task his originality imposed on him was more than enough for a lifetime. External stimulus came in the reiterated complaints of obscurity that reached him from friendly and unfriendly critics. In 1722 he supplied notes on the works of the two preceding years. In 1723 he was already casting his whole system into a fresh form.43 By the end of 1724 he was ready to publish two large volumes.

But he had no means of paying for such a publication. Intermediaries had interested a prince of the church in his writings. Some time early in 1725 Cardinal Lorenzo Corsini, to whom he had been advised to dedicate the work, offered to pay for its printing. It was passed by the ecclesiastical censor and all was ready, when a letter from Rome dealt Vico another stroke of disappointment. The cardinal, very politely and with the most friendly desire to be of service in the future, withdrew his promise. He had been visiting his diocese of Frascati and had discovered "many exorbitant expenses." Vico annotated the letter in these words: "Letter of his eminence Corsini, who has not the means of supplying the cost of printing the work that preceded the *Scienza Nuova*, whence I was obliged on account of my poverty to think of this last (the *Scienza Nuova*); for by reason of poverty I was restricted to print only this small book, taking off a ring which I had, a diamond of the first water and weighing five grains, with the price of which I was able to pay for the printing and the binding of the copies of the book; and being obliged by my promise I dedicated it to the cardinal."

These words cover one of the most heroic episodes in Vico's life. Rising from the blow that had been dealt him, he spent the autumn of 1725 in condensing the two large volumes into one small volume, and he paid for its production with perhaps his only precious possession. We should have a most inadequate idea of his effort if we regarded it as merely one of condensation. The two intended volumes were to have formed what Vico himself called the "*Scienza Nuova* in negative form," that is to say in the form of a destructive criticism of existing theories. He produced instead, with a fierce labour of mind (*aspra meditazione*), the *Scienza Nuova* as we have it. The manuscript of the negative version has been lost.

The only means we have of knowing what was in the lost work are a short account in the autobiography and a letter to Monsignor Monti, who had introduced it to the notice of Corsini. The first volume was to have discovered the principles of the Natural Law of Nations as involved in the principles of the "humanity" of nations. The discovery was to have been reached "by way of the improbabilities, improprieties and impossibilities which had been accepted rather by imagination than by reason." In the second volume were explained the genesis of human customs and the chronology of the obscure and fabulous periods of the Greeks, a chronology arrived at by process of reason, the Greeks being the source of all our knowledge of pagan antiquity. In the letter to Monti, Vico says he proceeds by way of confutation of his predecessors Grotius, Selden and Puffendorff.[44] Grotius, being a Socinian, fell into the heresy of primitive innocence and simplicity, Selden ignored all but Hebrew antiquity, and Puffendorf was responsible for the "scandalous hypothesis" that man had been cast upon the world without being helped or cared for. The errors common to all three writers were a failure to start from the belief in Providence, and the want of a consistent method of interpreting their authorities, at least as regards the obscure and fabulous periods and the earliest historical period. The principles of such knowledge are to be sought in those of sacred history. These principles are now established, together with the doctrines of Plato which support the belief in Providence, and which Vico defends, he tells us, against the Stoic doctrine of Fate and the Epicurean doctrine of Chance; also against Hobbes, Spinoza, Bayle and, finally, Locke, all of whom, by those very theories in which they oppose the civil maxims of Catholicism, destroy, in so far as in them lies,.all human society. Finally, accepting the Egyptian distinction of the epochs of gods, heroes and men, the above principles are discovered in the Greek fables, especially in that of Hercules which Varro had traced in the mythology of at least forty nations, exemplifying the uniformity of the laws underlying their development.

This work had already been put in hand for printing when Vico received the information that he would have no help from Corsini. In the letter which he sent on November 20th to that ecclesiastic, he tells him that he decided to abandon it on account of his advanced age —he was 57—and his uncertain health. He says he had intended in any case to employ the next year in writing a positive and shorter version. This positive and shorter version was now prepared in the hurry of two or three months and appeared before the end of 1725. It is the book on which the fame of Vico principally rests, the volume he carries in his hand in the Pantheon of the philosophers and men of science. Though we look in vain for any recognition of his importance by his contemporaries, he had no doubt whatever in his own mind as to what he had achieved. He knew that what he had to give mankind had not been given until November 1725 and that in that month he had in all essentials paid the debt which genius owes to humanity. He wrote to Giacchi, on November 25th:—

"I send my work to your Reverence with the love I bear you and the respect which is your due. Its reputation will be enhanced more in your solitude than in the most famous of the universities of Europe to which I have addressed it. In this city I know that it has fallen on barren ground. I avoid all places of resort where I might meet any to whom I have sent it, and if I do unavoidably come upon them I pass by with a hasty salutation. As they never give me any recognition that they have received my book, I am confirmed in my belief that here it has gone forth in a veritable desert."

His earlier works, he explains, were written in the hope of one of the higher chairs in the university. This last book he owes in a sense to the university, since by judging him unworthy of such a chair, it has left him the leisure to compose it. He would like it to be the only one of his works to survive him; all the others were merely a preparation for it. "Providence be for ever praised, since what appeared severe justice has turned out the supreme benefaction. For this work has invested me with a new manhood. No longer do I lament without reservation my adverse fortune and the corrupt mind of the age. That fortune and that mind have strengthened and aided me to accomplish this work. Thus (and if it be not true I wish it to be true) my work has filled me with a certain spirit of heroism, so that I am no longer shaken by any fear of death, nor have I any mind to speak of rivals. In fine, the judgment of God has set my feet as it were upon a rock of adamant, for he causes works of the mind to be judged by the esteem of the wise, who are always and everywhere few."

CHAPTER XIII

THE "SCIENZA NUOVA"

(1) *The Writing Of It*

THE *Scienza Nuova* of 1725 is a culmination. Opinions differ as to whether it is a greater work than the longer one into which he very thoroughly remodelled it five years later. But necessity had constrained him, in the failure of all assistance, to discard all superfluous polemic, and with sacrifice and concentrated labour to reveal the positive essence of his matured thought in its organic unity and powerful originality. Posterity owes a debt to Cardinal Corsini for his unwitting renunciation of a great honour.

Fifteen years earlier Vico had published his metaphysics, which was a philosophy of physics, a polemic against Descartes, an attempt to explain knowledge and Nature by a single formula. Two years had been given to the controversy thus aroused. Four years after this had ceased he was writing history, the life of Caraffa. About the same time the study of Grotius and perhaps the friendship of Gravina determined a concentration of his philosophical and historical meditations upon social institutions and the nature, origin and evolution of law. Caraffa was disposed of in 1716, and from that year to 1725 everything of consequence that Vico wrote was a more or less incomplete project of the *Scienza Nuova*. The inaugural oration of 1719, the synopsis and the juristic treatise of 1720, the two books *de Constantia* in

1721 represent the growth of the new science in his mind. Then in 1723 and 1724 he composed the two volumes of the new science in its negative and polemical form, which he was not able to publish. In the *Scienza Nuova* these works find their correction, development and co-ordination. The field is wider, and the exposition more systematic and proportionate. Everything now takes its place in a complete system set forth at moderate length. Philosophies of religion, law and poetry give place to a philosophy of man historically contemplated. The light falls no longer among rocks and chasms; it is diffused over a wide landscape. The change of language is also a great gain. The wintry dignity of Latin gives place to the sunny vitality of Italian.

In accordance with this very systematic treatment, the first book of thirteen short chapters affords a luminous introduction to the whole. In the first two chapters the scope and subject-matter of the science are made as distinct as anything so new could be made in so short a space. The next eight chapters are mainly devoted to explaining why the science has not been discovered earlier. They contain probably the substance, in a compressed form, of the lost "negative" version. The last three chapters explain the chief difficulties of the science, difficulties never previously overcome because not even suspected.

(2) *The Outline of the "Scienza Nuova"*

The hero of the story contained in the *Scienza Nuova* is the nature of fallen man. After he has turned away from the knowledge of the true God he still retains a certain sense of what he needs, and this, though obscured, is common to the whole race. This common sense is guided by Providence through necessity. It is a faculty of appetition and avoidance. In the *de Uno* it is defined as a common prudence of a community or nation by which all their members feel what is to be followed or shunned. In the second book of the first *Scienza Nuova* it is defined as "a common sense of each people or nation which regulates our social life in all our human actions, so that they accord in that which all of that people or nation feel in common." In a later version of the *Scienza Nuova* it is said to be "a judgment without reflection, felt in common by a whole order, a whole people, a whole nation or the whole human race." It is sometimes used in the plural as applied to different objects.[45]

Having lost its true object, God, it is still darkly conscious of immortality. But this sense of immortality is hidden in the recesses of the soul. Man in the face of death is conscious of a desire that there should be a power to overcome death on his behalf, a God superior to Nature. But having lost this God who, as superior to Nature, must be eternal and infinite mind, man in the face of death, and not only in the face of death, is curious to know the future. The common sense of the race thus gives rise to the false religions. There never was a nation of atheists. Men imagine gods and practise divination in order to know the future, which they think they can read in physical signs that convey the mandates of their gods.

Though their common sense does not give them truth it gives them shadows of truth. The belief in their gods and in the possibility of obeying them adumbrates the two truths of divine providence and the freedom of the will. This second truth implies that men have the choice to live according to justice. As common sense it produces the desire for law. In so far as a man's own passions are not involved he desires the rule of law. Here is the root of progress, the gate of man's upward way towards the life of reason, the basis of man's possibility of being man in the true sense and of realizing the divine idea of man. This desire of laws is therefore *humanity* in the specialized meaning Vico gives to the word. Its practices are governed by the three "common senses" of the human race. The first is that there is Providence, the second is that, through recognized offspring by recognized women, the principles of a common civil religion must be established. The third is sepulture. Any departure from these principles would be a sin against the common nature of mankind. Against such a sin the rites and ceremonies of all religions are precautionary. The consciousness of these principles and their preservation constitutes the "vulgar wisdom" of the human race, wisdom in Vico's system being either vulgar, popular wisdom, embodied in customs and early poetry, in religion and laws, or else recondite wisdom which is that of the philosophers and of developed reason.

Thus in the first chapter all the elements of the problem of the new science are given. The second chapter states the problem itself. This is the problem of accounting for the development, from those elements, of all the sciences, disciplines and arts of humanity to the degree of perfection they are capable of reaching, and have at least once reached, before beginning to decline. In attaining this perfection men confirm themselves in certain customs, to ascertain and establish which the vulgar wisdom comes, in the course of time, to be aided by the recondite wisdom, and practice joins reason.

This problem the ancient philosophers could not set themselves. The Epicureans were quite incapable of making any science at all of human affairs; they attributed everything to chance. Their interpretation was falsified by hedonism; consequently they made the rules of justice dependent upon a utility that was subject to perpetual change. The Stoics, certainly, believed in eternal, immutable justice, in the life of the soul after death and in righteousness as the true good. But they explained events by a fatal necessity; and they took away the essence of "humanity" by condemning all the passions and by making all crimes equal. By failing to recognize the importance of physical necessities and utilities, they ignored the whole process by which, through these, Providence has educated mankind. "The divine Plato" avoids all these errors, but even he does not conceive the true relation between abstract truth and historical development. Belonging himself to a philosophic age, he commits the "learned error" of supposing that the laws owed their origin to philosophic wisdom. His republic is therefore a purely ideal one. He does not see how Providence ordained matters for the world of nations.

In modern times Grotius, Selden and Puffendorf have written of the origin of laws. But the true problem has been concealed from these also. Even Grotius, who conceived and partly sketched a jurisprudence of the human race, is classed, not quite fairly, with those who attempted a purely utilitarian account of legal civilization.

Vico understood Grotius to claim that his system held good without any knowledge of God. The problem of understanding the work of Providence in leading mankind to reason was therefore not seen by the great Dutchman, to whom Vico elsewhere confessed so heavy a debt.

The philologers or historians have no better understood the matter than the philosophers. They give no credible account of origins. Their story hangs in the air. For want of a knowledge of the state of mankind before the beginning of history, the whole of history itself is misunderstood. The want of a true explanation is supplied by tales of impossible journeys made by philosophers like Pythagoras in lands separated not only by thousands of miles but by the "inhospitality of early nations." Vico has now completely abandoned the belief that the various countries derived their wisdom from a common early culture, whether Egyptian or Etruscan in its origin. Even in historic times the Tarentines had not heard of the Romans though they inhabited the same peninsula. The first Greek to get any historical notions of Asia was Xenophon. All the stories of Homer and others visiting Egypt in much earlier times are shown to be incompatible with known facts.

The true history of the human race is a history of its progressive mental states. The task of supplying history with its psychological basis, the great task which Vico set himself and his successors, thus revealing the presuppositions of any science of history, was seen by him, as its first pioneer, to be of immense difficulty. It could never be even approached by men who, like the Cartesians, valued only logic and worked only with ideas of mathematical clearness. It required an intense effort of imagination. It was necessary to enter into the minds of men divested of everything that civilized people take for granted, into the nature of men who had not even language. Even children are no guide to us here. A modern child at the age of seven has an enormous vocabulary. The geometrical knowledge involved in writing, in the formation of letters, is far beyond what is possible to a race of beings devoid of all abstract notions. Nothing travellers tell us of the most degraded inhabitants of remote, inaccessible wastes can carry us far towards the men who lived after the great dispersal. In this journey we meet with bitter uncertainties and desperate difficulties. We have to try to follow with our thought the beastlike wanderings of beastlike men, through the gigantic forest which was the world. The student of the new science is like Dante, who was met on the pathway towards truth by mysterious hindrances; and could not ascend into clearness until he had first gone down into the uttermost gloom and heard the desperate cries. "We wander," says Vico, "ignorant of the men and the places."

But one light shines continually through the long, nocturnal darkness, the unique truth that *this world of the Gentile nations was certainly made by men.* From this it follows that its explanation is to be sought in the mind of man. This positing of psychology as the basis of history and philology is one of Vico's greatest conquests in the domain of historical interpretation. The sentence has a further significance as a new application of his theory of knowledge. To have made a thing is to know it. It is no longer merely the unreal conceptions of mathematics that man is conceived as knowing, but the real institutions of social life. What was certitude, therefore, becomes truth. But this reconciliation of *certum* with *verum*, of authority with reason, is only achieved when history is narrated rationally, only therefore in the new science.

(3) *Ideas in History*

The two keys to the understanding of history are, for Vico, ideas and words. The second book of the *Scienza Nuova* reveals the philosophical approach, the third the approach by philology. The first idea to seize upon the primitive mind was the idea of a divinity which looks into the heart of man. This gives rise to conscience, religion and the necessary moral basis for society. In the use of the word "Providence" Vico is ambiguous. It means sometimes the power of God shaping events, sometimes the "common sense" of mankind that a supernatural being knows all their thoughts. This is not an insignificant ambiguity. The great step taken by Vico when he said that the world of nations is made by man, constituted an identification of the mind of man with the creative reason which knows because it has made. The human and the divine agencies in history are confused if Providence is both the divine power and man's belief in the divine power. Causation is still metaphysical and occasion physical. But then the mind of man is metaphysical. Man certainly lacks foreknowledge of how the divine plan will unfold. But if at each step he is identified with creative mind, he has appropriated the whole of the divine power, though the divine knowledge only becomes his gradually and in proportion as the work makes progress. One step is enough for him, but it is his own step. It is taken without knowledge of the distant scene, but its direction depends on natural necessities which, though provided by "Providence," are subject to psychological and physical Nature and its unchanging laws. Vico hardly escapes the pitfalls of contemporary deism and pantheism. On the one side is the assumption that physical nature, once created, works on independently, or by the power of an indwelling deity who has subjected himself to physical laws. On the other, the corresponding belief that the power of God has identified itself with the creative mind in man. We need not attribute to Vico the belief that the whole divine mind is involved in either physical or mental nature. He would certainly have ascribed omniscient foreknowledge to God and not to man. Spinoza believed that in thought and extended matter, which together make the whole of our universe, we know only two of the infinite number of God's attributes. Vico would have repudiated any kinship with Spinoza. But the philosophers of any one period stand outside the same doors, approach the eternal enigma by paths that are very close together.[46] Though not exact contemporaries, Vico and Spinoza were both dealing with philosophy in the condition in which it was left by Descartes.

The principal idea for Vico, as the student of human society, is the idea of justice. This idea is eternal and universal. Though eternal it has its course in time. The early brutish men have of justice only the seeds. What is eternal and immutable in the idea is the law of its unfolding and fulfilment in history. One of his examples is the history of the transfer of property. In the most ancient times the Athenians consecrated their whole estate (*campo*) to Jove. To acquire possession, permission had to be obtained through the auspices of the god. The law of the Twelve Tables at Rome marks a later stage. What was now required was a ceremonial and symbolic transfer, a clod of the soil representing the whole field. The validity of the transfer depended on strict observance of the legal form, as in the case of compurgatory oaths. Later on, all that was required was sufficient evidence of the actual transfer by the will of the parties. The principle of eternal justice underlying all these modes of acquisition was the principle of obtaining the consent of the former possessor. The development is from religion to philosophy, the gradual identification of authority with reason.

The order of human ideas with reference to justice is thus eternal. It is also universal because there is only one way in which it can everywhere be conceived as operating. Vico says it is impossible to think of the early brutish men as other than solitary, or of marriage having been initiated anywhere in any other than the way he describes. The same argument is applied to the origin of states and their development. With other illustrations from other aspects of history, from the development of war and religion, Vico enriches his exposition of how the eternal and universal idea of justice expands from a stage of obscure force, superstition, and rigid authority, gradually towards the recognition and supremacy of reason. Finally, all the time sequences he has been following are shown to be interwoven. The laws of a given time are not only the natural consequence of the laws of an earlier time. They correspond to and are conditioned by the religion, language and other social manifestations of their own time. They are all at any given time the diverse aspects and expressions of one mind at a particular stage. The *Zeitgeist* was first discovered, at least first analysed, by Vico.

One of his applications of the new science is too important to be omitted, his denial of the Greek origin of the Roman law of the Twelve Tables. The received story he pronounces to be completely incredible, and revealed to be so by the new science. Nobody who has made the terrible effort of dishumanizing himself, of crossing the dark, tempestuous waters of the primaeval terrors of men, and has entered into their mind, can suppose that the Roman plebs at the time when this event is supposed to have happened were capable of being governed by the laws of Solon. The plebs had centuries of tribulation and struggle to undergo. The new science rejects immediately the story of the famous embassy to Greece. It could have been believed only when the knowledge of early conditions had been lost, when history had become unintelligible for want of pre-history.

Vico's conception of history as the temporal expression of ideas that are eternal is not without difficulty. He claims that these ideas are "an ideal, eternal history which has its course in time." Inasmuch as he ascertained for the first time the organic nature of society and the normal conditions of progress, bringing order into a vast region of the most difficult problems where only a collection of narratives had existed before, Vico is one of the greatest pioneers of modern thought. But his conception of an eternal history as he states it is something more than a collection of generalizations however far-reaching and profound. Logically, as Signor Croce[47] points out, it would lead to a uniformity of development which is remote from the truth of history. By confusing the eternal idea with the actual series of facts Vico often makes his reasoning difficult to follow. An eternal idea of justice is one thing. An eternal history is quite another. It is part of Vico's conception of eternal history that it shows the gradual realization of the eternal justice. The principle of causality, as the condition under which the mind necessarily conceives the world of experience, might perhaps be regarded in a sense as eternal by contrast with isolated facts or events in the chain of historical causation. But its discovery does not give an "eternal" *history* distinct from, underlying, or causing the actual course of events.

(4) *The New Critical Art*

In the service of his new science Vico lays down the rules of a new method of research, which he calls the "new critical art." The general presuppositions of this art, the facts we are to bear in mind in approaching the problems of history, are that ancient historians adopted fables from motives of patriotism and in order to meet the demand of popular credulity, and, secondly, that in extracting the truth from these fables a certain order is to be observed in the application of tests. Where facts are doubtful we are to test them by their compatibility with the laws of the nation in which they are alleged to have occurred. When we are not certain about the laws we fall back on the mental habits of a people and on the climatic and geographical conditions of their land. If we had the history of a nation's laws, we should know that of their deeds; customs arise from men's nature, governments from customs and laws from governments, whilst laws give rise to civil habits and civil habits to the "constant public actions of the nations."

The critical art distinguished five kinds of historical evidence. The first is described as testimony contemporaneous with the birth of the gentile nations. This consists mainly of the fables, whose uniformity in many countries, separated by immense spaces of land and sea, proves the common mentality that invented them. Such are, for example, the fables of heroes born of gods and women. If Vico means that such fables are everywhere to receive the same interpretation, he is drawing a daring conclusion from their wide distribution. It is difficult to see what else he can mean.

The second species of testimony is the hieroglyphic nature of all early writing, revealing the concrete, imaginative, simple character of the minds that made use of it. Next come two classes of physical proofs on whose general nature Vico is not very explicit. He merely says of the first class that there is nothing in nature to contradict the statements about giants which we find in the Old Testament and in various human records. Vico had formed a theory about these giants, a theory whose originality perhaps gave it a disproportionate importance in his eyes. The text about the sons of God and the daughters of men having an offspring of giants has nothing uncanny for him. Here is no "woman wailing for her demon lover." The sons of God are not fallen angels but the descendants of the righteous Seth; and the daughters of men belong to the unsanctified race of Cain. The children of such mixed marriages were likely to be neglected, to grow up without cleanliness and without the fear of the schoolmaster. Cleanliness and fear diminished, Vico believed, the human stature. Their absence in the Germans of Tacitus produced again a tall race of men. Perhaps the importance of this quaint theory lay for its author in the link it afforded between sacred and profane history.

The second "physical demonstration" starts from the supposition that for a long time after the flood the earth was too damp to send forth those fiery exhalations which, when ignited, become thunderbolts. This occurred in different climates at different epochs, with the result that each people had its own thunderer, or Jove; their mythologies developed independently at different times from similar causes acting on their common nature. A solitary exception to this mutual independence of origins in the matter of divination and early science is admitted in the case of the descendants of Seth and of the Chaldeans. Each of these appears to have been blessed with vestiges of a higher truth, truth far sunk from its divine source but superior to the first guesses of other tribes. The stellar divination of the Chaldeans was superior to the corresponding science of the western peoples. Some astronomical knowledge even passed from Chaldea to Egypt, Greece and Italy.

The fifth and last weapon in the new critical armoury consists of what its discoverer calls "metaphysical proofs." These, as we might expect, are psychological. One is the anthropomorphic tendency in early religion. Men, finding in Nature powers they did not understand, ascribed to

them their own characteristics and motives. The first
and most sublime metaphor invented by man was that
the whole universe is a vast, intelligent body speaking
with real words, words that are things, the phenomena
of Nature, a language like the primitive language of
gesture among mankind before even hieroglyphs were
inscribed.

(5) *Applications*

One of the earliest problems to which these principles
of research are applied is that of the origin of property
in land, or, as Vico calls it, the division of fields. The
errors and difficulties have all arisen from assuming that
when the division occurred political society already
existed. This mistake would never have occurred if it
had been remembered that the Cyclops in the *Odyssey*
had already their private land around their caves and
lived there separate and solitary long before the beginnings
of social life. Vico's solution we have seen. The first
division of lands is inseparable for him from the first
sepulchres.

The origin of the state is the next problem. This, too,
has already been dealt with. The key to its solution lies
in the relation of the "heroes" to the "clients." In no
other way can we understand the existence of two orders
in the political community from the very first, and the
fundamental importance of the tension between the
orders throughout its history. The heroes are one of
Vico's most magnificent historical reconstructions. As
definitely as Carlyle he rejects the notion that force and
fraud account for the great things in history. The basis

of the heroic character is magnanimity. Their superstitious religion was not imposture but the necessary
first stage in the honest interpretation of Nature. Under
the stress of this tremendous religion they became chaste
and strict in the morality of the family. They were pious
towards their ancestors. Necessity made them industrious
in cultivating the soil and courageous in defending it.
They were generous in protecting the refugees from the
wilderness.

But Vico has no idyllic belief in primitive innocence.
These men were not far from the rough and simple
beginnings of "humanity." They are the rude fore-
fathers. Their religion originated in fear, and the chief
quality of their greatest god is power, crudely conceived
as physical strength; with all gods and men pulling at
a chain, Jove could overmaster them, could haul it up
and them too, with the Earth they stood upon.

To these heroes the refugees who became their clients
were at first not men, having no part in "humanity,"
but beasts or things. "Wherefore one must cease to
marvel at Ulysses' treatment of the dearest of his associates, Antinous, when, for merely failing, and that with
good intentions towards his master, to obey instructions
blindly, he (the said Ulysses), mounting into a heroic
rage, wanted to cut off his head; or at Aeneas, when
he desired to offer a sacrifice, killing his associate
Misenus."

Another piece of early psychology set right by Vico
is the assumption that the love of fame was the motive
for the exploits of early heroism. The primitive champions
were far other than historians in a self-conscious civilization believed. Their true motive was the safety of the

order of things to which they belonged. Narrow as this conception was, it was their contribution to progress. Vico holds very clearly the belief that the ruling powers of any age owe their stability to their contribution to progress, and fall when they cease to accord with the ideas that lie at the root of their superiority. Demoralization overtakes the race of heroes. They become luxurious, idle and oppressive. When this happens, the revolt of the plebeians is certain. It is followed, however, as has already been shown, by the foundation of the state, of the aristocratic monarchies. In the rivalry of the orders patrician virtue revives. It is this rivalry, in which the plebeians strive to deserve and to acquire the privileges of "humanity" and the patricians to retain their own dominance, that leads to the greatness of Rome.

Arrived at the foundation of states, Vico explains all history in the light of Roman history. He had studied Roman law all his life and was by profession a teacher of Latin rhetoric. Roman history best illustrated his new science, the survival of origins, the slow transformations of custom, the gradualness of institutional change. The Athenians developed so rapidly and altered their laws so frequently as to elide many interesting transitions and efface the traces of growth. Other nations for other reasons tended to diverge from the normal course dictated by the "ideal eternal history having its course in time," but differences in mental ability are a principal factor. The Romans were not an over quick or clever folk. Their pious preservation of old formulas gave occasion for the ingenuity of legal fictions and for the very gradual expansion of the seeds of truth and justice.

Everywhere it is a law of expansion. "Humanity" is

first slowly recognized in the plebeians, then in the conquered provincials, until later Roman law expresses the supremacy of universal reason. It is the same in Vico's surprising anticipations of modern Homeric geography. He sees the traces of a great expansion of the field of Greek exploration and colonization. Stories originally written about quite small areas in Greece and the Aegean were shifted at length to the farthest shores of the Euxine and westward to the portals of the Atlantic. A strong imaginative realization of change in the human outlook and its scope never forsakes him. Vico was one of the most historically minded men who ever lived. Looking at the heavens, the early watchers first attached importance to the fixed stars. This is inferred from these stars having the names of the oldest gods.

Vico was not the first to attempt to apply general principles to history. Bodin, for example, had examined the geographical factor. But, compared with Vico's, all earlier attempts are slight. He is in nothing more admirable than in his clear realization that the science immediately underlying history, the science through which the roots of history strike down into other sciences, is psychology. On this psychology of history, of which he is the founder, calling it metaphysics, he bases the history of morals. He sees a progress from rough, physical, solitary or primitively social standards towards the rational, humane and political civilizations, followed by a decline towards luxury and a selfish individualism, in which "in the great multitude of bodies their minds retire into their original solitude."[48] The sequel to this is either the recurrence of barbarism or conquest by an uncorrupted nation.

(6) *Philological*

According to Vico, history is to be studied in ideas and in words. The reason why the growth of language and the truth of fables have not been understood is similar to that for which Selden, Grotius and Puffendorf failed to discover the true beginning of laws. The intellectualist fallacy lay at the root of the error in both cases. Plato and Aristotle, Scaliger and Patrizzi assumed that the makers of primitive speech or song were thinkers like themselves and like the poets of their own time. Vico spent twenty-five years of unsparing concentration on the problem before he could place himself, by a final triumph of imagination, beside the simple, rough beings who first, after the great dispersal, uttered human speech.

He necessarily repeats himself here. He had dealt at greater length with the whole question in 1721, and the history of words cannot be separated from the history of ideas. He sees in the poetry, that is, the fables of early men, an interpretation of their rudimentary notion of Providence as operating in physical nature but still more in human destinies. Mythology is thus explained aetiologically rather than euhemeristically, though solutions of the latter kind are not excluded. The sky is a vast body with a soul and speaks in thunder, but also "those who helped the human race by inventions were looked on as gods."

Vico has now constructed a system of myth-interpretation corresponding to the new critical art in the history of ideas. First he explains "monsters," such as the satyrs and goat-footed Pan. The explanation is essentially the same as that given four years earlier of the fables in general. The "monster" is the incarnation of a proposition, the joining of a predicate to a subject. The satyrs are the savages who have not learned chastity. Speakers incapable of abstraction conceived lustfulness concretely in the likeness of a lustful animal. When this quality was to be posited of a man, a being had to be imagined who was half man and half goat. Similarly the second "principle" explains metamorphoses. Having no adjective by which to say that Daphne became stationary, the poets turned her into a plant. Families which acquired a fixed habitation became stocks or stems. Incongruities like the crop of armed men from the sowing of dragon's teeth are accounted for in the same way. This fable "contains a long period of history." The Earth, conceived as a living being, most resembles a snake or dragon. The sowing of its teeth represents agriculture and an agricultural community can support armed warriors. Wings are a very important symbol because of their association with the sky, therefore with auspices and the right to take them. Only patricians could take the auspices. Pegasus, the winged horse, meant that nobles alone fought on horseback, and Vico reads with delight that, among the American Indians, the nobles alone adorn their heads with feathers. It was only in a very late and corrupt fable that the wings of Saturn had anything to do with the flight of time.

This corruption or change of fables is in itself an important "principle" of interpretation. The lyre and its chords had once had other meanings, very different from their common use in later myths of Orpheus. A process of specialization had taken place. The chord once meant any kind of bond. It meant the bonds of obligation between human beings. The sum of such bonds is the state. Hence Orpheus and his lyre appear at the foundation of cities. Gold meant first coin; then anything yellow; lastly, by specialization, the yellow metal. The first meaning gives us the golden age as the discovery of agriculture. Only in late and "corrupted" myths does the golden age mean a time of ease and security. In the sowing of corn Ceres goes to the underworld. So Aeneas is guided thither by the golden bough. This last example is taken from Vico's earlier work, but it is a very characteristic piece of the new science.

(7) *H o m e r*

For some years Vico had given much attention to Homer. The notes which he published in 1722 contain an elaborate study of the life reflected in the *Iliad* and the *Odyssey*. Homeric theory is an important field of application for the new science. Homer is found to belong to a third age of poets. The first poets had no special, poetic language. They belonged to the generations of men who created language, and the first language was all poetical. The first poems were not the creation of individuals but of whole peoples. In the second age of poets the old myths and meanings had become corrupt and partially lost. It is the third age which first sees individual poets, men who consciously seek poetic material in the fables which had formerly been a folk language. Since Homer belonged to this period he is discovered to be an individual.

Vico denies that there is anything primitive about

Homer's prosody. The verses of the earliest men, who uttered their feelings with awkward slowness under the influence of religious fear, were iambic: "Iō paiàn, Iō paiàn, Iō paiàn." If dramatists after Homer wrote iambics, it was because of the religious origin of the drama. Homer's metre was essentially of later origin. He had behind him a long age of development and the slow deterioration of a great epoch. Hence the decadent morality of his gods and the great difference between his fables and their original meaning in the first language. But he was a reformer. He set himself to restore religion by showing, in the *Iliad* the long train of woes following upon adultery, in the *Odyssey* the contrast between the wisdom and endurance of Ulysses and the wickedness of the suitors. He was not too far removed from the first times to have the use of a language essentially poetical and sublime. Nor had he any other wisdom or philosophy than civil wisdom, that of the early communities. It was an age when men still lived by the senses. Two passages in the *Odyssey* show that reflection was still an unknown faculty. They are those in which the wise counsels in the minds of Telemachus and Antinous are spoken of as sacred and occult powers. In Homer there was still a very vague conception of long periods of time, so that a war of ten years was a perpetual struggle, such a war as barbarians wage, without any previous declaration or subsequent treaty. Vico thinks the Trojan war was of this character. When, in the tenth year, a treaty for single combat is made, a great period of savagery has ended, and a great period of international relations has begun.

(8) *Ages of Language*

Corresponding roughly to the three ages of man according to ideas are the three ages according to language—divine, heroic and human. Men, having lost speech, recommenced communication by means of signs. A certain pose of the arm signified reaping; its repetition indicated a number of years. The names of anthropomorphic gods were a very early vocabulary. Saturn, for instance, was the harvest. According to Varro there were thirty thousand gods in the "first" language of ancient Latium. The heroic language, which came next, has already been exemplified. It involves such primitive generalizations as the extension of names like Hercules or Theseus to mean the race of heroes or the whole of mankind in the heroic age. It is the great period of the fables. The "human" language is in comparison highly abstract, with its phonetic alphabets and its analytic method of denoting objects, indicating qualities and, finally, of expressing ideas. Though these three languages, roughly speaking, follow each other in chronological periods, no clear demarcation is possible. Traces of an earlier language tend to linger, especially among uncultivated people. A Florentine peasant even in Vico's time will still indicate three years by saying, in the poetic phrase of his ancestors, that he has thrice reaped his crops.

The history of speech, like the history of ideas, shows recurrence. The middle ages repeat the Homeric age, not only in feudalism but in poetry; the age of Dante is again a heroic age. If Dante is inferior to Homer, it is largely because he is imbued with philosophy. Vico is sure that, had Dante known nothing either of scholasticism or the Latin language, he would have been a greater poet. Even so he is far above Virgil, who is a poet by art and learning in an unpoetical, "human" age. Heraldry, with its mute symbols, is another example of recurrence. Its real significance in a civilized period is found in the coins and flags of the nations, which, having still the same relation to each other as individuals had in earlier times, have no common speech but that of pictures. So in Herodotus, the Scythian Idantura sent to Darius a mouse, a frog, a bird, a plough and a bow. By these signs he claimed the water, the auspices, the soil and the defensive arms of his land.

(9) *Conclusions*

At the end Vico recurs to the general principles of his new science. Applying them to the history of language, he arrives at "the Idea of a Dictionary of mental expressions (*voci mentali*) common to all the nations." His list of the fundamental ideas of the patriarchal age is intended as a help towards this. In every language of the heroic period everywhere there were the same twelve things to be expressed, gods, the family, the heroic order, auspices, sacrifices, the unlimited power of the father, courage, magnanimity, fame (not apparently excluded), sovereign dominion of the soil, military command, legislative authority. Returning thus through words to ideas, we recover the unity of the problem. Vico ends with a wide survey of history. The culture, the *humanitas* developed by each nation separately is not lost when that nation loses its independence. The conquered become plebs, with the interest of plebeians in natural equity, which is the sum and climax of the whole progress of law. The levelling effect of monarchy, seen at its best in the Roman empire, makes it the form of government most suited to the "human" age when the seeds of truth have become the final fruit of equal well-being. Providence has so ordered the affairs of nations that in their ultimate and truest manifestation of ideas and of justice the laws are found to be in accordance with the highest human reason. Though Plato had no understanding of the primitive conditions, and therefore was not in possession of the "new science" and could not explore the ways of Providence, it is Plato's philosophy that humanity finally rests in, not the fatalism of the Stoics nor the casualism of the Epicureans, but a philosophy which sees a divine mind in the ordering of the world. Platonism is for Vico the point at which human wisdom comes nearest to Christianity.

CHAPTER XIV

LIFE AND WRITINGS (1725–1729)

A GREAT book, changing the course of speculation or removing unexpectedly to a great distance the landmarks of discovery, sets the leading minds of the world everywhere upon fresh tasks and alters the whole orientation of intellectual activity. Such consequences followed the publication of the *Meditations* of Descartes, the *Monadology* of Leibnitz and the *Principia* of Newton. The new science of Adam Smith affected the policy of statesmen in his own generation. The new science of Vico did nothing of the kind. There is no greater contrast in the history of the mind than that between Vico's inner consciousness of what he had done and the outer traffic in the small change of petty compliment and adulation in which he found himself engaged immediately afterwards. It was as if a great ship had been built, capable of navigating all the oceans of the world, and was left moored in the dock of the shipbuilder to be visited occasionally by a few friends of the inventor, and mentioned in their correspondence by one or two superior persons who recognized not so much its value as the cleverness that must have gone to its construction.

The most distinguished of these superior persons in Vico's case was Antonio Conti, who has his own important place in the philosophy of letters and the literary intercourse of nations.[49] It was he who in 1728 persuaded Montesquieu, then on his travels in Italy, to buy a copy of the *Scienza Nuova*.[50] Conti met Montesquieu in Venice. The next year the great Frenchman was in Naples. He certainly bought Vico's book, but so far as we know he never took the trouble to see Vico. A copy was sent to Newton. It might as well have been dropped into the sea. No notice was taken of this book by Leclerc, though he had given so much attention to the *Diritto Universale*. The only place where the *Scienza Nuova* was appreciated to any purpose was Venice, where a small group of distinguished men, Lodoli, Porcia and above all Conti, encouraged its author to further efforts. It is to them in part that we owe Vico's autobiography and the second *Scienza Nuova*.

Nothing irritated Vico more than to hear on all hands the complaint that the *Scienza Nuova* was obscure. In general he thought this either a device of his enemies to cause its neglect, or an excuse for not reading it. It was not only his enemies, however, who found it obscure. There is an anecdote about it similar to those told of Browning's *Sordello*. Nicola Capasso no sooner began to read it than he felt he must have lost every spark of intelligence.[51]

Vico's letters during the years between 1725 and 1730 are full of the depression of mood produced by this absence of recognition. It almost appears as if his judgment of his age was affected by it. He understood that the age of Descartes and Locke was not propitious to his own work. He foresaw that the age which followed was likely to be influenced largely by the schools of thought whose tendencies he considered most harmful, and he believed that the decay of a civilization begins with wrong thinking on the part of philosophers. The neglect of the languages of Greece and Rome, the languages of religion and law, was to him one of the worst signs. He compared the writers of his own day with those of what he considered a decadent period of Greek thought and he saw in a rising scepticism the precursor of that individualism which was to dissolve the bonds of society and bring about the next recurrence of barbarism. To say that Vico was driven to think thus because his *Scienza Nuova* was not well received would be absurd. There is little in these letters that he had not said before, even as early as 1708. But it all surges up in his mind and goes down on paper in his complaint of the neglect of his great work. It was not that the work did not sell. It was fairly soon sold out. It became dear. But it was not the less unappreciated. One of his friends, the brother of that Nicola Solla who became his first biographer, told Vico himself that the *Scienza Nuova* seemed less admirable than the oration which Vico wrote on the death of Angela Cimini. Vico's answer[52] is extremely courteous and kindly. He certainly ventures to differ from his friend as to the comparative importance of the two works in question, but he admits that if the oration were an example of true eloquence it would deserve the highest praise, since true eloquence is wisdom speaking, and the three glories of man are heart, mind and speech. He sets down again for Solla's benefit his objections to the new critical science of the age, and its neglect of human for mathematical studies, as though the young were to be sent out into a society consisting of lines, numbers and algebraic signs.

During the same year in which Vico finished and published the first *Scienza Nuova* he wrote his autobiography. Count Govanni Artico di Porcia at Venice had the idea of procuring and publishing for the guidance and encouragement of studious youth a number of autobiographies by famous learned men, and Vico's among them. Vico says he only agreed to write it after much urging. Write it, however, he did and with his accustomed celerity.[53] Porcia was pleased with it, as well he might be. It is certainly one of the great autobiographies of the world. Porcia and his friends Lodoli and Conti insisted on using it as a model for the guidance of the other autobiographers, in spite of Vico's protests against a proceeding which he feared, and perhaps not without reason, might expose him to envy.

One reason for the success of Vico in this by no means easy department of narrative is the definiteness of his purpose. Porcia's idea was to assist youth by showing them how to find a secure path through their studies, as Descartes wanted a philosophy to enable him to take such a path through life. In his letter of September 1725 Porcia wrote that Vico had understood his object better than any of the others. Vico's own account is that he wrote his life "as a philosopher, meditating causes both natural and moral as well as the occasions of fortune, and why even from childhood he had felt an inclination for certain studies and an aversion from others, what opportunities and obstacles had advanced or delayed his progress, and lastly the efforts which, guided by certain principles he had acquired, availed later to make fruitful his ultimate reflections on the subject of the *Scienza Nuova*. Such and not otherwise he conceived his literary biography should be." In short, it must be a genetic explanation of the *Scienza Nuova* in which his life had found its meaning and importance.

The passage quoted, it has been observed,[54] indicates that the autobiography is the New Science applied to the life of its author. The leading conceptions are certainly there, the efforts, the distinction between cause and occasion, the growing clearness of the principles guiding him, the use of these principles in showing the meaning of the events, the overruling Providence and the conclusion that such and not otherwise on these principles it must have been. Many times has Vico used these very expressions in concluding some investigation regarding the social conditions of long past ages. The reader of these pages has had ample opportunity of judging the great value of the autobiography for the understanding of its writer's life and work. In all probability the students of the *Scienza Nuova* would have been far fewer than they have been had Vico never written his own life. It is difficult to imagine what one's studies of Vico would have been like had one not possessed the autobiography, which was included among the portions of Vico's work that Michelet selected to translate.[55]

The chronological and other inaccuracies matter comparatively little. What matters more is the omission to acknowledge certain influences in adolescence, particularly that of the Cartesians of Naples in the early nineties of the seventeenth century, and the omission of such names as Bruno and Campanella. These deficiencies have been conjecturally supplied.[56] Even if the dawn of certain ideas is antedated by Vico, the fact remains that he does give us in the retrospect the connection of those ideas, if not in all cases with the reading out of which historically they arose, at least, with the authors and principles on which in his philosophy they were based.

And this is what Vico must have meant in using in his autobiography language that suggested the methods of the New Science. He used the principles of his mature thought to explore his own past. That is not the same thing as attributing to his early manhood the philosophy of his middle age. What he says is that his early studies gave him the direction of his later ultimate discoveries, that the combination, for example, of the philosophical with the philological interest in his adolescent legal studies was contributory to the elaboration of a philosophy which took account of history, the discovery of an eternal law having its unfolding in time.

Ferrari complains that the autobiography does not give to Vico's life, as the *Scienza Nuova* gave to the life of nations, a psychological account of the growth of ideas.[57] But the book is very far from being devoid of psychological interest. The self-revelation is, on the contrary, one of its most remarkable and admirable features. The invalid child, with titanic intellectual pride, with a Faust-like mental energy and ambition driven inward by the weakness of his physical condition, by the sensitiveness of his temperament and the depressing poverty of his family, yet working on in the subterranean mazes of a heroic self-education, compensating by lonely intellectual victories for the denial of conquests in the world of action and fame; the austere singleness of purpose and laborious yet fervid achievement of his tasks; finally the assuagement of bitterness in the realization that his disappointments in the matter of academic promotion had fulfilled the design of Providence, the

177

completion of the great work that set his future glory upon an adamantine rock; all these phases of his wonderful but outwardly stagnating existence are manifest in the autobiography.

Disappointed of understanding and recognition, Vico had the mortification of seeing his principal work belittled and misrepresented in one of the chief literary organs of Europe, the only one that seems to have taken any notice of it. In London no notice was taken, though copies of the *Scienza Nuova* had been sent to Newton and Conyers Middleton. In Paris the *Journal des Sçavans*, in spite of Conti's connection with the literary world of France, gave no sign. A copy had been sent to Amsterdam, but Le Clerc unaccountably failed to notice it. Only the *Acta Eruditorum* of Leipsic inserted a brief and defamatory comment.

This appeared in 1727. Vico's account of the occurrence is given in his autobiography and in a letter to Giacchi. A person whose name cannot be discovered by us, though it was known to Vico, sent to the *Acta Eruditorum* information of the publication of a work called *Principi d'una Scienza Nuova*, which was not the full title of Vico's book. It was represented as having been written to flatter the prejudices of Catholics, as being published anonymously though known to be by a certain Abbot Vico, directed against Grotius and Puffendorf and more in accordance with the author's own mind than with the truth; finally it had been received even by the Italians with disgust rather than approval. The volume of the *Acta* containing this slanderous little review had reached Naples early in 1728, but its author, who possessed the copy, had kept it under lock and key.[58]

Even when it became known and was mentioned to Vico by one who frequented his home in the evenings, he did not at first realize its nature. When at last he read it, it seemed to him clearly the work of an enemy. In fact, he says he knew who his enemy was and refrained from publishing his name because he did not wish to bring upon him the penalties which his offences against church and state had incurred. But he did publish a defence,[59] couched in a tone of severe indignation against what he regarded as a crafty attempt to prejudice readers against his book and to mislead them as to its authorship.

The only part of the *Vindiciae* which is still of interest is a short digression on the nature of laughter. It arose from his opponent's statement that Vico had indulged his *ingenium* at the expense of truth. For Vico the *ingenium* is the faculty by which truth is discovered. Without any real occasion for it he goes off at this point into an examination of the nature of the ridiculous. Those who possess *ingenium* to a high degree are acute and perceive the whole truth about a group of things. These, the best minds, do not find things ridiculous. Demosthenes, the greatest of orators, was unable to raise a laugh. But the second-rate minds, which are *argute* and see things partially or superficially, give rise to what is humorous. The physiology of laughter is in the surprise of the nervous system when the mind, intent and expectant of an object congruent and adequate to its antecedents and environment, is suddenly presented with the inadequate and incongruous. The fibrils of the brain and nerves are shaken by the disappointment, and laughter is the result. Wise men do not deal in the ludicrous because they see things steadily and whole. Brutes do not laugh, because their consciousness contains only one thing at a time and cannot compare what they expect with what they receive. The humorist is half-way between sage and brute. A low kind of humorist, he who is not merely a laugher but a derider, is he who sets out to distort things so as to arouse laughter in others.[60]

An Italian oration which Francesco Solla indiscretely pronounced to be Vico's masterpiece was published with a collection of verses by the friends and admirers of Angela Cimini, Marchioness of Petrella, who died in 1727. The friends of Vico, though not able to understand his work, must have been at least a congenial circle. His daughter, Luisa Vico, whose dowry he gained by writing the life of Caraffa, had rewarded the care which the philosopher had lavished on all his children. She was a poetess and the friend of other women who play an interesting part in the intellectual life of Naples. Among these was Angela Cimini. A distinct group was formed for literary discussion, meeting often at Vico's own house. Among those who for a time belonged to it was Metastasio, who addressed sonnets to Luisa Vico and received from her sonnets in reply. Angela Cimini, besides writing poems, was an ardent student of philosophy, taking lessons in Platonism from Doria and in the philosophy of history from Vico himself. We have in Vico's oration a vivid and pleasing picture of the meetings of his literary friends, and of this impulsive, delicate lady of genius as the centre of it. A comparison of the intellectual society surrounding Vico in the earlier years of his work at Naples with the people who now came about him gives the impression of a distinct difference of tone and manners. The influence of women seems to have been very small in that Naples of lawyers and ecclesiastics who haunted the bookshops and libraries and formed academies under the Spanish viceroys at the end of the seventeenth century, though Burnet had already noticed some differences in this respect. The eighteenth century had now dawned in earnest. Vico's friend, Doria, had now written a book to prove the intellectual equality of the sexes, the manners of the French court had taken more and more hold on Italy in spite of the political predominance of Austria, and the *salon* was taking its place in the life of Naples.

From his pupil Nicola Solla, who, making use of the autobiography, wrote a short life of Vico soon after his death, we have a description of him as he appeared in his lecture room two hundred years ago: "Infinite was the concourse of youths who, besides the precepts of rhetoric, drank from his lips the milk of universal wisdom. He took all opportunities of interpolating the most instructive reflections in every branch of knowledge. At home he condescended to explain Plautus, Terence and Tacitus; . . . penetrating the most secret recesses of the heart, he sought to discover the springs of human conduct, and passing on from duty to duty according to our various relations to God, to ourselves and to other men, he went on to draw the outlines of moral philosophy and of the universal law of nations, brought out more clearly, and practically illustrated, in the acute reflections of Tacitus." A hostile writer said it was dangerous to attack Vico during his lifetime, since "a great part of the city would have rushed in to defend him, as they had been in youth initiated by him in the art of oratory," and so the rash critic would have been "censured in every company." This can only mean that Vico was beloved by his pupils, or at least so much respected by them as to make any attack on him appear a proof of bad taste. His own attitude to them was essentially sympathetic. The fourth inaugural discourse contains these words: "So far are these exhortations to the study of the worthy arts and sciences from being a mere business of pomp and ceremony, that whenever I see—and I see it daily—youths of tender age, who naturally shrink from toil and incline to games and sports, who have nevertheless passed the long, silent hours of night in serious meditation and come in the early dawn wet with rain or shivering and numbed with cold to hear their teachers, then, so love me God as, rather than see them despond, I would do all in my power to confirm their minds with repeated exhortations."

"He was of medium height," Solla tells us, "of an adust habit of body, his nose aquiline, his eyes lively and penetrating, and from their fire it was easy to conceive the power and energy of his vigorous mind. His choleric temperament contributed to the sublimity and swiftness of his intellect. He loved his intimates with an excess of tenderness, preferring a respectful friendship to servile fear. He was discreet and indulgent in censure, sincere and liberal in praise. If attacked, he defended himself, but always within the bounds of decency and equity.'"

CHAPTER XV

THE SECOND "SCIENZA NUOVA"

FROM about 1718 to the time when he ceased to be capable of work, all Vico's most serious efforts were devoted to the elaboration and correction of the *Scienza Nuova*. The edition of 1725 was scarcely printed before he had begun to write additions and amendments, which, before many months had passed, provided material for a far larger volume. The pressure to republish came from Venice—from Lodoli, Porcia and Conti. The Venetian resident at Naples had bought all the remaining copies of the original edition to meet the demand of his friends at home. Lodoli found a printer in Venice who was willing to undertake the work, and wrote to Vico for permission at the end of 1727. His request was supported by Porcia and Conti. The scantiness of Vico's ordinary correspondence seems to be indicated by the fact that only by a chance information did he hear early in 1728 that letters for him had been for some time lying in the post office in Naples. His Venetian friends asked him to make any additions to the original work that might occur to him.

They received a bulky manuscript which constituted essentially a new work. The printing was commenced in Venice and the forthcoming publication was announced at the end of the autobiography, which was not printed until 1728. The Venetian publisher wished to produce an edition of all Vico's works, and tried to procure them from the Neapolitan publisher by the device of fictitious private collectors. The trick was discovered, and the author declared that the only one of his writings which he desired should survive him was the *Scienza Nuova*, about to appear in a new form in Venice.

In the autumn of 1729, however, Vico broke with the Venetian publisher and demanded the return of his manuscript, though the printing was more than half done. He gives, as the reason, that the Venetian, considering that Vico, having twice announced the early appearance of the work, would be unable to retire from the undertaking, pressed him with unacceptable conditions.

After recovering his manuscript, he set himself to rewrite it once more. The new book was written between December 25, 1729 and April 9, 1730.[61] He had much to alter in the book of 1725. In particular he thought he had done wrong to divide it into two parts, one dealing with ideas and one with language, since his main theme was the combination of these two. This in itself would have involved a thorough recasting of the book of 1725. Vico had, moreover, by this time drastically modified his theory of Homer. Nor did the work of 1730 prove to be his final recast. The ultimate edition was in 1744, the year of his death. But he had been deeply disturbed by the prevalence of a disposition among his readers to regard his theories as unintelligible, due, he believed, in some cases to hostile intent, though he admitted the great difficulty of the subject.[62] He was led, therefore, not merely to develop his ideas, a process imposed on him by their novelty and vast scope, but also to try ever fresh methods of explaining them. The second *Scienza Nuova* bears, in its arrangement, the marks of this preoccupation. He prefaced it with an allegorical picture, and devoted a long introduction to the explanation of the objects depicted. This involved a complete and compressed account of the whole subject, the whole new science. The first book is similarly, in part, the explanation of a chronological table which obliges him again to go over the whole ground from a different point of view. He then gives a long list of what he calls axioms. There are one hundred and fourteen of them. Few deserve to be called axioms. They constitute another discursive presentation of the new science. Only when he comes to the second book, that is on page 156 of Ferrari's first edition of 626 pages, does the author recover the analytic method of exposition which had served him so well in the first *Scienza Nuova*.

These devices did not make for lucidity. It is likely, however, that the form thus given to the work reacted upon its matter. The compressed restatement of the whole subordinated the facts more and more to the theory, fusing together the history and the philosophy. The second *Scienza Nuova* therefore bears to the first the same relation as the first bears to the *Diritto Universale*. Theory becomes more systematic, criticism is pushed further in the destruction of all that stands in the way of theory; more characters, hitherto received as historical, are resolved into myths, and the greatest of these is Homer. Vico had at his disposal, when he hurriedly rewrote the *Scienza Nuova* between Christmas 1729 and Easter 1730, a great store of notes and memoranda excogitated in the course of his continual revisionary labours. He had all the material of the *Scienza Nuova* in its negative form, which had been severely compressed when turned into the positive

Scienza Nuova of 1725; and he had been again preparing his book for the Venetian press on a very considerable scale. So he had ready to hand many new examples and new ways of putting things. All this helped to make the second *Scienza Nuova* a fresh book. As he desired to put into it everything by which he wished to be estimated by posterity, he did not shrink from again giving the old material wherever the new form allowed its use. But the new form in itself leads often to greater fullness and depth. Mere variations of phrase are very suggestive. When we now read of the "substantial unity" of the law underlying all national systems of legislation, we see the influence still exercised by Vico's early studies in Platonism or even in scholastic realism. On the other hand, there are flashes of modernity. Contrasts in the Athenian character (sensitiveness and delicacy, for instance, broken by outbursts of vindictive passion) are explained as Nietzsche explains them and as Burchardt explains the same contrast in the Italy of the Borgias. The philosophers had accelerated culture in Athens at a pace too swift for a fundamental change of disposition.

The severe compression of the first *Scienza Nuova* would have left us in doubt on important questions. How far, for example, was Vico conscious of the contrast between his so-called first and second theories of knowledge? The second *Scienza Nuova* makes it clear. The new philosophico-historical science has far more reality, we now read, than geometry. Like geometry it is built up of elements which the mind itself makes. But human actions are real, whereas points and lines, surfaces and figures are not.[63]

There is a new analysis of the poetic wisdom which

constituted primitive and heroic culture. We are now asked to read separate chapters on the poetic metaphysics, the poetic logic, the poetic morality, the poetic theory of the family (oeconomica), the poetic politics, physics, cosmography, astronomy, chronology and geography. The poetical metaphysics is in turn analysed as (1) a civil theology of Providence; (2) a philosophy of authority, successively of primitive religion, of the family, of the larger families or *gentes*, of the senate, the plebs and the state; (3) a history of ideas; (4) a critical philosophy of the authors of all these and especially of the earliest of them; (5) an ideal, eternal history common to all nations; (6) a system of natural right and (7) a universal history. Amid much repetition fresh things continually occur. The figures of speech receive a younger brother in "irony," which could not have belonged to the early language since it involves the power to reflect. The history of early Greece and Rome is now treated more critically.

Solon's individuality begins to be shaken in 1730. It is altogether disintegrated in 1744. His name has become that of a general type like Hercules.[64]

Vico must have lived intensely in his primeval forest and its clearings, his theories as to what happened there are so distinct and elaborate. The second *Scienza Nuova* contains a complete history of the invention of the different parts of speech. Nouns were invented before verbs, and children use them far earlier; the ideas they awaken leave the most distinct traces on the memory. The first modifications of these ideas give rise to particles. "But verbs signify movements, which involve 'before' and 'after,' which are measured by the indivisible of the present moment, which even philosophers find it hard to understand."[65] An apoplectic patient, whom Vico knew, could easily make use of nouns but had forgotten all his verbs. When verbs did appear they came in the imperative mood. The patriarchs used speech sooner than the subject members of their families and their speech was command.

The poetical logic is now enriched by these and other supplements and corollaries. The episodes of Homer are "born of the clumsiness of the 'heroic' minds, which did not know how to extract the essence of the story; we still find it in idiots and in women." As a proof that song is easier than ordinary speech we now have the example of an excellent tenor singer, whom Vico knew personally; when he found it hard to utter a word he broke forth into a *soavissimo canto*. The political interpretation of the poetic language is rather perplexingly complicated by duplication. Since the plebeians followed their masters, though at some distance, in the acquisition of the successive qualities and rights of humanity, the gods who had signified the achievements of the former came to stand secondarily for the latter. There is now a second Saturn and a second Jove. This gives rise to far-fetched interpretations. The desire of Saturn to devour Jove is true of the plebeian Saturn and the patrician Jove. It means that the plebs wanted to devour the authority of the patricians.

The reader is now again warned not to attribute ideal virtues to the heroic peoples on account of their name. The word is obviously taken from the tradition of an age of heroes before the dawn of history. The heroes certainly achieved much in taming the earth and its primeval monstrous growths, but their virtues were for the most part not ours. In an absolute ethical sense they were often not virtues at all. They corresponded to a stage of life at which force, even brutally exercised, was the most divine quality, bringing them nearest to the divinity before whose terrors they bowed. This "heroic" virtue long survived. Vico, a lover and observer of children, takes his example from the Spartans, "the unlettered Lacedemonians" who best preserved the "heroic" customs in Greece. Their treatment of infants and boys suggests in him a contrast with "the delight we now take in our young children, constituting all the delicacy of our nature."[66] He observes in the *Iliad* a complete absence of the sentiment of romantic love. Achilles shows no trace of any such passion for Briseis, nor does Menelaus for Helen. It was certainly not her beauty that launched a thousand ships. She was a "poetical," that is a general character, a myth to signify the victims of early piracy.

The third book as a whole is entitled *The Discovery of the True Homer*. Homer was far more studied than Dante in the Italy of Vico.[67] The Homeric problem reappeared in a form familiar to the ancients. D'Aubignac had denied Homer's individuality four years before Vico's birth and had reckoned forty Homers, but his essay was not published until 1715. He had accepted from Josephus the ancient tradition that the poems were for many generations unwritten, and had pointed out the impossibility of a long sequence of minstrels knowing both poems by heart. There is no evidence that Vico owed anything to d'Aubignac. His own friends Caloprese and Gravina and his contemporary, and in some respects complementary fellow historian, Muratori devoted much attention to Homer, nor was it perhaps without effect that, in 1723, appeared the first complete Italian translation, that of Salvini. Gravina's views resemble Vico's on some points, though, like Caloprese, he was more interested in the nature and value of the poem than in its authorship or the mentality of Homeric man.[68] He does, however, say that the savage character of the heroes must be explained by that of their times.

Vico now recapitulates the substance of his earlier writing, laying stronger emphasis on the extreme vagueness of the traditions regarding Homer's life, birthplace, age and literary character, on the lack of a biography, on the great variety of incompatible social conditions portrayed in different parts of the two poems, and on the popular, and in the Vichian sense "poetical" character of the conceptions of the universe and of society. In accordance with his whole doctrine of early wisdom he rejects absolutely the philosophical meanings read into Homer by late Greek writers. Having carefully prepared the reader he arrives at his own conclusion, artistically reserved to the end, that Homer himself is, at least in part, a myth, a "poetical" character.[69] "All these things reasoned by us and narrated by others concerning Homer and his poems, without our having intentionally aimed at any such theory—since the most acute and learned readers of the first *Scienza Nuova* did not perceive any such drift in it—lead us now to affirm that the same thing has happened to Homer which happened to the Trojan war, of which the best critics affirm that though it represents a famous epoch of time, it never in the world of fact took place. And certainly if, as of the Trojan war so of Homer, great vestiges did not remain, such as are his two poems, the great difficulties would lead us to conclude that he was only a poet in idea, but never a man really living in the world of nature. But such and so great difficulties, together with the poems of his that remain to us, seem to force us half to affirm that this Homer was an idea or a heroic character of Grecian men in so far as they told their history in song."

Though Vico is only led "half to affirm" his theory, his facts leave very little room for individual authors. We cannot help sharing his surprise that he was so long in arriving at the dissolution of Homer, and that neither he nor his acute and learned critics drew the fatal conclusions from the first *Scienza Nuova*, in which, if nothing else, the most heterogeneous elements were discovered in the poems. It need hardly be pointed out how all this makes Vico the precursor of the "folk song" theories of Herder and others that played so great a part in the creation of nationalistic ideals at the end of the eighteenth century and the beginning of the nineteenth.

This solution once reached, all difficulties and objections disappear. Homer's birthplace was found in various parts of the Greek world because the whole Greek world was Homer. He lived at different periods because he was the whole heroic age of Greece. As all the doers of the time were Hercules, all utterers of the poetic speech were Homer. Vico had an intense admiration for Virgil. But though Virgil may have had the highest genius possible in man, he was not born to the natural use of the sublime, poetic language, in which the ancient rhapsodes had so great an advantage in imaginative diction, so great a disadvantage as regards abstract thought in comparison with all writers of later times. Not until the Greco-Roman civilization had fallen into ruin, not until spoken language had almost been lost among men and been driven to start afresh with symbol and monstrous metaphor, will it be possible for Dante to repeat almost the miracle of Homer, without, however, ceasing to be an individual.

The fourth book is a summary of the whole *Scienza Nuova* in the form of an outline of the career run by the nations. It is full of new examples, recasts and recombinations of old syntheses, flashes of insight anticipating the historical conclusions of the nineteenth century. Several pages are given to discussing *Reason of State*, with its precursor in the esoteric jurisprudence of the patricians; their common basis in *salus populi*, and their common disregard of private interests. *Reason of State* does in the interests of policy what equity does in the interests of justice. In democracy, which makes for publicity and natural equity, it is neglected or at least discredited, but it finds its place again in the cabinets of monarchs.

Vico's doctrine of the recurrence of the whole cycle of historical periods receives most elaboration in the later versions of the *Scienza Nuova*. One consequence is that we have now much more space devoted to the middle ages. He finds his theories amply confirmed in the history of mediaeval institutions. In fact, readers of Stubbs in our day have little advantage over Vico in essential understanding of compurgatory oaths, trial by battle and the other "theocratic" sanctions of barbaric justice. He not only saw the resemblance between the middle ages and the pre-classical period of Greece. He saw their chief differences. Above all, he grasped the infinite importance of the separation of church and state, with its cause in the growth of the Christian Church as a persecuted community under the declining Roman Empire.

This is set forth in the beginning of the fifth book, to which Vico appends the "Conclusion of the Work," bringing the whole into the philosophical perspective of the Eternal, Natural Commonwealth ordered by Providence. It is an evolution of man from body to mind, from force to reason and justice, first under the stress of the physical needs and fears of the individual, then under the educative tension of the struggle for equal rights in the state. At last, when false philosophy, and when decaying virtue, when the corrupt forms of religion which set the highest rewards in physical enjoyment have led to the downfall of civilisation, humanity proves itself a phoenix and arises from its ashes.

CHAPTER XVI

LIFE AND WORK (1730–1744)

IN 1730 Vico was sixty-two years old. Such happiness as it was given him to enjoy in this world was drawing to an end. His best years were probably from 1726 to about 1733 or 1734. There was little outward prosperity; there was no adequate recognition; there was much toil and some mortification; there was the beginning of incurable illness and of the exhaustion of energy. But the battle to fulfil the great work of his life was won. In two forms he had published, in 1725 and 1730, the thoughts which proved him to be among the few greatest thinkers in the age of Leibnitz and of Newton, and he knew what he had done though his contemporaries did not know it. His narrow home was the meeting place of a circle of friends comprising some of the best minds in Naples.[70] His oldest intimate companion, P. M. Doria, mathematician, scholar, philosopher and poet was still among them. There were Brancone, later to hold important office in the state, and the eloquent friar Michelangelo da Reggio; there were pupils of Vico, like Solla and the poet de Angelis, above all his own daughter, the poetess, and her friend Giuseppa-Leonora Barbapiccola, poetess and student of philosophy. Though Vico had enemies, among the more narrow-minded clergy, who perhaps, however, did not misjudge the ultimate implications of his work, he was well fortified as regards ecclesiastical friendships, though the cardinal to whom he had dedicated the first *Scienza Nuova*, and who as Pope

Clement XII accepted the dedication of the second, was somewhat negligent in his patronage and cool in his gratitude. Nor had philosophical polemic embittered his relations with the philosophers of the Cartesian school. He was highly valued by Caloprese and by Spinelli; both of these had Platonic tendencies and neither shared Descartes' contempt for the ancient classics. Spinelli was among the distinguished men whose sons were in the number of Vico's private pupils,[71] and having eagerly read the second *Scienza Nuova* he sent its author a letter of praise and criticism which was received with appreciation and evoked a reply of some length. In June 1730 Vico was in correspondence with Muratori, who had informed him of his nomination to the academy of the *Oziosi* at Urbino. Vico thanked him and sent him a copy of the *Notae in Acta Lipsiensia*. Though the Venetian friends who had encouraged him may have cooled after his withdrawal of the half-printed manuscript in 1729, he had a zealous admirer in the professor of metaphysics at Padua, Nicola Concina, as well as in his brother Daniele the theologian. But in contrast with prosperous friends, Vico was a man burdened with poverty and with an amount of drudgery that few would have found compatible with the highest energies of the mind. If we compare his burden of obscure toil with the freedom of his greatest contemporaries, Newton, Leibnitz or Locke, to give their best time to their discoveries, we see in the lack of fructifying leisure and of freedom from care one of the most remarkable aspects of his heroic life.

The clouds began to darken around the ageing philosopher very soon after the publication of the second *Scienza Nuova*, but not before his influential friends had been able a little to relieve his poverty. A great European war, nineteen years after the treaties of Utrecht and Rastadt, changed the government of Naples. The Bourbon King of Spain was married to a princess of the house of Parma. Elizabeth Farnese had never ceased intriguing to secure the succession of her son to the old possessions of her family. In 1733 Spain grasped an opportunity to restore Bourbon rule in Naples. France in that year went to war with Russia and the Empire to secure the Polish crown for the son-in-law of Louis XV. Spain joined France with a view to her own anti-Austrian ambitions in Italy, and Philip V, girding his son Carlos with the sword he had himself received from Louis XIV, sent him forth to conquer Naples. The conquest was an easy one. The Austrian troops were outmanœuvred on the frontier in 1734. With the Spanish fleet in full view of the capital, the populace, discontented with Austrian rule which had been expensive, and reassured by a proclamation of Carlos as to their one cause of anxiety, the Spanish Inquisition, frightened the Austrian viceroy Visconti from the palace and the city. The representatives of the city went forth to offer the keys of Naples to the new king at Maddaloni. They found a typical Bourbon. After receiving their allegiance, Carlos spent the rest of the day in shooting the pigeons that nested in the ducal palace.

But Carlos did not bring with him only the depraved tastes of the decadent Bourbon race. He had in his train the young Pisan lawyer Bernard Tanucci, the Italian Turgot. The age of benevolent despotism and rationalism had dawned for Europe, and was reflected in the new régime in Naples. It was represented there by Tanucci and later by Filangieri, the legal reformer who, in 1787, showed

Vico's masterpiece to Goethe. The new government gave the kingdoms of Naples and Sicily independence of foreign sovereignty for the first time since the end of the fifteenth century; Carlos was a younger son and was not expected to be king of Spain. Whatever might be the faults of his government, it would not at least have to support a host of foreign officials or supply the means of empire to Madrid or to Vienna.

Vico was among the first to benefit, though in a humble way, by the political change. Carlos entered Naples in May 1734. A natural appendage to an independent monarchy was the office of Historiographer Royal, which had not existed in Naples under the Austrians. In June Vico made application for this employment. His application was supported by Celestino Galiani who, the aged Vidania having at length gone to his rest, was now *Cappellano Maggiore*. It is clear from Galiani's letter to Montalegre, the Secretary of State, that Vico was now recognized as an illustrious citizen and teacher who was growing old without adequate recognition, whilst he was in sore need of it in a substantial form.[72] The application was successful, but it took a year for the appointment to be made. Vico, in his own petition to the king,[73] claims to be the oldest of all the professors. "Prostrate at your royal feet," the illustrious suppliant pleads that no year has passed without "some work of his poor intellect" having seen the light of day, that a catalogue of these works can be consulted in the Venetian collection of *Opuscoli Eruditi*; that Vico's contribution to this collection, his autobiography, was circulated as a model by the editors to the other contributors, who were the leading writers of Italy. He pleads further that among the works enumerated in the said catalogue is a panegyric on his majesty's royal father Philip V on the occasion of his visit to Naples; also a book on the *Principles of Universal Law*, which "Bernardo Tanucci, that illustrious writer, now your Secretary of Justice, with whom your petitioner never had any correspondence, declared in a Latin dissertation in 1728 to be the first work ever issued in Italy upon such a subject." Vico mentions as well the laudatory review of Le Clerc, and, coming to the *Scienza Nuova*, selects Conti as the best witness of its importance. "And now your petitioner finds himself weighed down with age, with a numerous family and very poor, with only 100 ducats of salary from his academical chair and a few trifling fees incidental to his duties." Therefore he prays for the office of historiographer, so that, uniting its emoluments to those of his chair, he may have peace in which to chronicle his Majesty's very glorious deeds and end his life honourably.

The office of historiographer gave Vico, from 1735 onwards, another hundred ducats. In the same year the new government signalized its reforming character by setting up a commission to examine the state of the University. It included Montalegre and Tanucci, its president was Celestino Galiani, and it raised Vico's professorial stipend to 200 ducats, giving him thus in all 300 ducats a year, a poor income as prices went then, but an enlargement of ease to a man who had been used to living on a third of it.

Vico was by this time unable to bear all his burdens, to which was added the domestic trouble of a son in whom weakness of character led to dissipation, vice and public disgrace. It is not certain whether this son was

Philip, born in 1720, or Ignatius, born in 1706, nor in what year Vico, one of the gentlest of fathers, felt obliged to apply to the public authorities for the imprisonment of his son to prevent worse trouble. The story told by Villarosa is that when the police came to arrest the unfortunate young man, the father rushed upstairs before them, calling to his son to escape. The son, Philip or Ignatius, was imprisoned for a considerable time, being released on showing signs of amendment. Ignatius lived with his wife in the paternal house and had a daughter. He died in May 1737, leaving his wife and his father as her joint guardians. Two months later Vico forbade his daughter-in-law the house and fought a lawsuit success-fully for the custody of the child.

The final ruin of his health began in 1731. As a child, quite apart from his famous accident and its results, he had been regarded as consumptive, and one reason of his accepting the appointment at Vatolla was this real or supposed tendency. Later he went by the nickname of Doctor Tizzicussus. In the supplement which he added in 1731 to his autobiography he mentions a disease which had consumed his palate.

The mainstay of his later years was his son Gennaro,[74] who was born in 1715. In him, as in his sister, the paternal seed of classic and philosophic learning had fallen on fruitful soil. Gennaro first assisted with the private teaching in Vico's own house. Later he used to save his father at the university the labour of dictating the passages for comment. The son would read out the passages and the father would explain them on another day, thus minimizing the number of times Vico, whose legs, apparently through some kind of nervous trouble, were none too good, would be obliged to drag himself to the university. One day Gennaro felt the desire to make the comment himself; "with trembling and palpitation" he did so. He told his father what he had done and found that the explanations he had given were satisfactory. He was encouraged by the *Cappellano Maggiore*, Galiani, to continue taking his father's place. This must have been in 1736. He tells us he had been lecturing for four years when the proposal was made in 1740 that he should succeed to the chair, whose duties it was clear Vico must renounce for ever.

The old philosopher was in friendly hands. At the instance of Galiani he appealed to the king to allow the substitution, describing himself as overcome by weariness and by the struggle with straitened circumstances, and as almost confined to his bed by disease. Gennaro had given good proofs of his fitness. He had satisfied the *Cappellano Maggiore* for four years, beginning when he was not more than twenty-one. There is also a letter from Nicola Concina recording the extremely good impression he had made. The application was promoted in the Council of State by Brancone, Vico's old literary friend, now minister for ecclesiastical affairs. The only doubt seems to have arisen from Gennaro's expressed desire to combine his work with practice at the bar. Galiani insisted that the chair of rhetoric, "a much esteemed and not easy profession," would require him to give all his time to the study of eloquence. The council granted the petition and Gennaro Vico became professor of rhetoric in 1741.

The years after 1730 were by no means empty of literary toil on Vico's part. It was not until 1736 that he ceased almost entirely from revising the *Scienza Nuova*. Two sets of notes, called by their author *Correzioni, miglioramenti e aggiunte* were produced in 1730, a third in 1731 and a fourth before the end of 1734. These were incorporated in the edition which was written in 1735. This was occasionally retouched until 1743 and published in the next year, too late for its author to see it in print. Though the alterations are numerous, there is no such recasting as gave the second *Scienza Nuova* a form so different from that of the first, nor do the changes show any important modifications of the leading ideas.75

For the first few years after the publication of the second *Scienza Nuova* Vico maintained a considerable miscellaneous literary activity. He still took part in collections of complimentary and occasional verse. He was still in demand for prefaces and inscriptions. He was still consulted by authors about their works. The most interesting of his *obiter scripta* in this period is the *Judizio sopra Dante*, a brief essay applying the historical theories of its author and expressing an appreciation of Dante as a poet not commonly felt in the early eighteenth century. It is a subject of dispute whether Vico owed anything to the advance in critical principles made by Gravina.76 He must at least have felt some increase of confidence in finding that his friend rated Dante far more highly than was general in the age of the Arcadians.

"The comedy of Dante Alighieri," commences Vico, "is to be read from three points of view, as the history of the barbarous age of Italy, as a fount of the most beautiful Tuscan speech, and as an example of sublime poetry." Vico reminds the reader of his principle that the early poets are historians, Homer being the greatest. History, like all other sciences of the time of Dante as well as of that of Homer, was conceived poetically but truthfully, since the barbaric or heroic age was void of reflection and therefore of deceit. What Homer was to Greece, Ennius was to Rome and Dante to mediaeval Italy. He tells the truth about his characters in the *Divine Comedy*, mythologically and poetically, with that combination of actuality and fable that constitutes poetry, and he differs from Homer in that he writes conformably to the Christian religion and its doctrine of a future state, with its threefold vision of the hopeless, the hopeful and the blessed spirits. Vico controverts the theory that Dante collected his vocabulary from all the dialects of Italy. Not the lifetime of one poet but the organized research of an academy would have been required for such a task. The mistaken theory arose from the number of words that were formerly common to several dialects and from the adoption later of that of Tuscany as the standard in other provinces. This claim by the dialects to a part in Dante is paralleled by the claim of the different parts of Greece to be the birthplace of Homer.

Finally, considering Dante as a poet, Vico says, like Bruno in the *Eroici Furori*, that sublime poetry is not to be learned by any rules of art. Homer was preceded by no Longinus. The two sources of poetry are loftiness of soul and a knowledge of the great, public virtues, above all of magnanimity and justice. For this reason the Spartans, who were forbidden a literary education, quite commonly uttered sentences such as poets rarely achieve, and achieve only when writing at their best. Dante owed the sublimity of his speech to his epoch, when barbarism, a "heroic" age, was drawing to a close, and the human mind, long fallow, was prepared for plentiful harvests. The *giudizio* is very short, and does not give so much of Vico's opinion on Dante and on poetry as may be collected from the second *Scienza Nuova*.

In writing a preface for some poems of de Angelis in 1730, Vico was serving an old pupil and friend to whom he had already communicated his ideas regarding poetry. The preface is interesting for developing the theme that nobody has been great both as poet and as orator. Eloquence belongs to the age of democracy, of rationality and of all that is clear, popular, on a level with the average mind. Poetry, on the contrary, is the language of the heroic age and is rooted in the obscure sublimities of a religious conception of the universe. Vico is rightly regarded as in some ways the precursor of romanticism. In pointing out the intrinsic opposition between rhetoric and poetry he goes beyond the romantics, beyond Hugo and Byron, whose rhetoric is now reckoned to them as a fault. He anticipates the present time.

As need hardly be said, Vico had certainly no contempt for rhetoric or eloquence. It was one of his principal accusations against the Cartesian philosophy that it had withered the sources of oratory by reducing thought to the driest terms. He regarded eloquence, as he regarded the comedy of Menander and Terence, as the glorious expression of the age of reason. Cicero and Demosthenes owed everything, he considered, to Plato, and the Academy.[77] This is the theme of one of the latest of his minor works, a discourse in which he took occasion to compliment the new literary society founded by N. Salerni on choosing for their censor "Paolo Doria, a mind of rare and sublime intelligence, most celebrated among the learned of this age for his many works on philosophy and mathematics"—a final tribute to a very old and close friend.

This was in 1736, the year in which Gennaro began to assume, not yet the responsibility, but the labours of the professor of rhetoric. In 1738 Vico—the historiographer royal could hardly do less—produced an oration for the marriage of the King with Maria-Amalia of Saxony-Poland. It certainly shows failing vigour, otherwise he would have sketched the causes and the course of the war of the Polish Succession with the same energy with which he had treated that of the Spanish Succession in the funeral oration for d'Althann's mother. He is content to touch the theme briefly, emphasizing the great extent of the area covered by the war, and expressing the fear lest, had it gone on longer, it might have exhausted the human race. The old man was either treating the subject with perfunctory rhetoric or he had really been painfully impressed by the news of sieges and battles and the wastefulness of the tragedy. He is treating a favourite theme in suggesting that the now reconciled houses of Spain and Saxony should turn their arms against the Turk. There had always seemed to him a natural opposition between two civilizations based on different religions.

In 1740 and 1741 occurred the business of transferring the chair to Gennaro. In 1742 the old professor excused himself from the task of criticizing a work sent him by its author. He was still preparing for the publication of the third *Scienza Nuova*. The last letter we have of him is dated on the last day of the year 1743, and concerns its dedication to Cardinal Acquaviva, three weeks before

Vico's death. The letter must have been written during the brief recovery mentioned in the following account by Villarosa of the final illness. "The aged philosopher became daily more feeble, and he ceased to remember the names of the commonest objects around him. He no longer enjoyed, as he had done at the beginning of his illness, the Latin authors whom Gennaro, with affectionate devotion, read to him. He passed whole days sitting quite silent in a corner of his house, and taking very little food. He scarcely even saluted the friends with whom he had been accustomed to converse on themes grave or gay. Nothing could be effected by the remedies which his medical colleagues at the university prescribed. The unhappy Vico at length did not even recognize his own children whom he tenderly loved. He remained in this most miserable condition for a year and two months, and was at last confined to his bed, with invincible repugnance for all food, drinking slowly and painfully of the waters of death. Some days before breathing his last he recovered his senses, and as if awakened from a long sleep recognized his children about him. But his only benefit from this recovery was the knowledge of his approaching end. Seeing for himself that all human remedies were useless, he sent for Father Antonio Maria di Palazzuolo, a learned Capuchin and his intimate friend, to receive from him the last friendly offices in the moment of passing. With the most perfect submission to the Divine will and a prayer for the pardon of his sins, comforted by the powerful aid of the Church which he had eagerly requested, continually reciting the psalms of David, he died peacefully on the 20th of January, having passed the seventy-sixth year of his age."

Years before, he had said that misfortune would follow him even after his death. If so, it was a strange prophecy of a scene which prolonged the shadow of external misery beyond the last hours of one whose whole life had been an example of intellectual and moral greatness on a background of poverty and struggle. The right to bear the pall was disputed between professors of the university and the members of the confraternity of Santa Sophia, in which Vico was inscribed. The body was left in the courtyard of the house, until Gennaro, applying to the cathedral clergy, obtained burial for his father in the Church of the Oratorians, which Vico had attended. Only in 1789 was Gennaro able to place an inscription on the wall of the church.

CHAPTER XVII

THE GREATNESS OF VICO

THE aims of the present work are those of biography and exposition rather than of philosophical criticism. To trace, however, the origin and growth of such a body of thought as Vico's would have been impossible except in the light afforded by the subsequent development of knowledge and speculation. There is no biography without interpretation, even had the subject of it been less idiosyncratic than our hero; and for clearness of interpretation even the humblest biographer must assume now and again the functions of criticism and estimation. It remains to unify and to supplement the impression afforded by those scattered reflections.

To do this is the more important for the reason that nothing could be more false than to regard Vico as merely one of those singular geniuses who, by applying their acuteness in various departments of thought, have made remarkable anticipations of later discovery. To leave the reader with an impression that the writer of the *Scienza Nuova* had forestalled Wolf and Niebuhr and had reached conclusions in philosophy in which was prefigured the teaching of Kant, would be to present an enumeration in place of a synthesis. His work did not consist of scattered achievements performed more successfully by later scholars better equipped because of the progress of science. Had it been so, it would have little significance now.

Most great thinkers have been deeply imbued with the

culture of their own age and have explored the foundations of its thought in order to deal with its unsolved problems. Vico did likewise, but he did much more. His own age seemed to him, in its typical representative, to have confined itself to establishing a method of infallible procedure in the sciences susceptible of exact calculation and analysis, and to have substituted a recognition of experience for the problem of reality. His own method was the opposite of that of Descartes. Instead of emptying his mind of all previous systems, he sought their synthesis, in so far as he believed them to contain truth, and this in him was not an eclectic but an organic process.

He therefore necessarily set himself different problems from those which occupied men who had identified themselves with the mind of their own age. This self-educated man had profoundly experienced in himself the mind of the past in three great epochs or vast regions of study. He had pondered the nature of man as revealed in the development of speech and the difference of languages; comparing the phrases of Dante, Boccaccio and Petrarch with those of Virgil, Cicero and Horace, pondering the hieroglyphics of Egypt and the savage symbolism of Scythia, and studying with Plato the origin of names. Secondly, he had studied the problems of mind in the light of idealist philosophy from Plato to Giordano Bruno, seeing in Platonism the nearest approach to what he held to be the true religion. Finally, he had occupied himself almost from boyhood with the problem of justice, and of man as a social being, since he had seen from the first in legal history a philosophical study. These three worlds of mind were for him not merely three fields in which to accumulate knowledge, but three reflections of

eternal truth. But what gave him at length his own interpretation of eternal truth, his own original philosophy,
was, after all, the impact of his own age, with its particular
questions and its provocative rejections and limitations.

For he belongs essentially to modern times. So far as
he was concerned, Descartes had not lived in vain,
however inadequate he thought Descartes' answer to
fundamental questions. He was post-Cartesian. Descartes
had made the problem of knowledge what it was to
remain for a century and a half, the central problem of
philosophy. Vico's own treatment of this problem is the
core and commencement of his philosophy. And this
treatment was doubly due to Descartes. It was due to
what Descartes gave him, to what he found wanting in
Descartes and to the relation ultimately established
between these two.

What Descartes gave was the assurance that we know
whatever we cannot doubt, our own existence therefore,
since in thinking we cannot doubt that we think and are.
To Vico this was merely a subjective certitude, and
inferior kind of knowledge, lacking its basis in eternal
truth. It was long, however, before Vico could supply
anything better. He did not for that reason acquiesce
and work on, or attempt to work on, from Descartes'
position as from a sure commencement. He sought an
independent basis in more than one way. In the first
place, with the Aristotelian test of science as a knowledge
by causes, he conceived that to know a thing implied
having its causes in oneself, being its maker. This gave
him only a test of knowledge about unrealities, the point,
the line, the unit of geometry and arithmetic. He was not
satisfied.

o

He had a second independent basis. He could not prove it, but he believed Plato was somehow right in supposing Providence had endowed the human mind with metaphysical truth. Vico did not think he could prove the existence of God. But he was clearly not satisfied to admit that man's knowledge of God is on a level with Descartes' certitude of his own existence. Nor did he speak of it as faith in what we cannot know. We have seen that in 1710 he had recourse to poetry in order to give some idea of what an English poet calls the "shadows of celestial light."

Some time before 1725 he conquered a new realm for true knowledge. This world of nations with their languages, laws, arts and governments was most assuredly made by man. Man has therefore true knowledge of reality in the whole sphere occupied by himself and by the whole race to which he belongs, with all its works and ways, institutions and beliefs. Vico had found a second and more valuable basis of knowledge, independent, that is, of the subjective certitude of Descartes.

In building on this basis the whole Vico was employed; the Platonist, the philologist and the jurist. The Platonist believed profoundly that the ultimate reality was mind. God was pure mind, wherein were all causes. In his first inaugural oration Vico had preached from the text "know thyself." The knowledge by man of his own mind, a simulacrum of the divine mind, was the key to the knowledge of the universe. This line of approach to the problem of knowledge, combined with the doctrine that the whole world of nations was made by man, explains the pantheistic point of view which Vico was always avoiding as the rock to which the whole current of his thought was bearing him. God is mind; man is body and mind. The created world is known only to the creating mind, to God only, therefore; and the world of nations is most certainly made by and known to men. The divine and human mind must not be identified. The human mind is therefore a simulacrum of the divine mind. Perhaps when Vico wrote this he considered all the knowledge which self-knowledge gives to the human mind to be only a simulacrum of knowledge. But when he had come to see that the world of nations is most certainly made by man, he did not regard man's knowledge of that world as merely a simulacrum of knowledge.

In one respect at least Vico was consistent in repudiating pantheism. The universe could only be explained as mind, divine or human, with one reservation. There was a residuum. God is pure mind; man is mind and body. Vico certainly believed also in body. And it is precisely of body, in his philosophy, that we have not true knowledge but only certitude. For he divided the universe into three; the metaphysical world of God, the double nature of man and the physical world. The physical world is altogether made by God, and God alone has true knowledge of it, man knows it only in so far as his mathematical figments apply to it; of the physical world in itself he has only certitude.

But it was the historian and philologist Vico who knew that certitude was not to be despised. He approached history, the history of the world of nations, from both ends. At the beginning, in the great dispersal after the deluge, man was brutish, immersed in body; and a very concrete imagination, very full of passion, was the beginning of man's mental work. At the other end of the long epic of history was the world of justice, of equal good, of reason and philosophic truth. Man lived for ages under authority, by certitude, by imagination, poetry and the religion of physical force embodied in the Jove who was the strongest of gods and in the heroes who were the strongest men. Reason was present here only as a seed whose expansion was to be the slow work of time. The contrast between the two kinds of knowledge, between certitude and eternal truth, the vulgar wisdom and the rational wisdom, was the outcome of Vico's reaction against Descartes. It was also the origin of his philosophy of history. It revealed to him the necessity of history as a distinct manifestation of mind; it revealed the philosophical character and justification of historical study.

Vico was the first man to have this conception. He was the founder of the philosophy of history. Voltaire has the credit for being the first writer to speak of a philosophy of history. But Vico only missed it by an accident of phrasing. "There has hitherto been lacking," he wrote, "a science which should be at the same time a history and a philosophy of humanity."[78]

To recognize a philosophy of history we must conceive the whole of history as a form of reality whose laws, conditions and ultimate aim if it have one, are not to be resolved into the laws, conditions and aim of any other aspect of reality. For example, if the aim of history, the final good of it, is merely the practice of virtue by human beings, then, so far as concerns ethics, there is no special philosophy of history, and history brings nothing to ethics which is not present in ethics however conceived and quite apart from history. If the laws of history are those of economics, sociology or even psychology, then history as a whole, the total destiny of man unfolding itself in the course of time, admits of no special philosophy. But if there is something in history not explained by these laws, if, taken as a whole, it requires an explanation different in kind from the explanation of any of its single aspects—as different as metaphysics is from aesthetics— then we are right in speaking of a philosophy of history.

With his belief that the maxim "know thyself" is a key to every kind of knowledge and with his inveterate Platonism, Vico regarded history as a rational process, a process in which the substance was mind and the form was reason. Since the substance in which the historical process takes place is mind, the laws of history are based on those of psychology. This Vico clearly understood, though the word psychology was invented after his time. All the same, the laws operative in history are not merely those of psychology, if history as such is to have a meaning. And Vico did see in history a manifestation of mind which, though analogous to that which can be studied in the individual man, could not have been discovered from such study alone.

In order to understand Vico it is necessary to make use of his own science, to put ourselves back into a time when the boundaries of different sciences as we have them were not yet marked out, and many of our scientific and philosophical terms either were not yet invented or had meanings different from those given to them now. For want of distinctive words his ideas require some effort to disentangle them. The terms he uses to explain the manifestations of mind in history fail to distinguish the spheres of epistemology, psychology and ontology. It was not that Vico did not distinguish them in his own mind. But partly from a strong tendency to synthesis, and partly because the new science lacked a sufficient terminology, the meaning of such terms as *autorità*, *certo*, *vero*, is continually expanding or contracting. The exact translation of the *Scienza Nuova* would be a work of the greatest difficulty.

The English words "authority" and "certitude" scarcely convey the sense required for an understanding of the earlier phases of mind in Vico's view of history. Moreover, *certum* is a part of *verum*, and the earlier phases expand gradually into the later as the human will becomes rationalized. All customs and institutions are modifications of our mind; in these modifications they have their origin; therefore their origin constitutes their nature and by it they are to be understood. Yet the true nature of man is only seen when customs and institutions have been moulded by the complete unfolding of the seeds of truth and reason. The individual is only to be understood through the history of society.

The knowledge possessed by men in the early and heroic ages, immersed as they were in the senses, ruled by traditions arising out of a religion of fear, by rigid customs and the letter of a harsh law, was not a rational knowledge by causes, consciously arising from rational creation of that which is known because created by the knower. It was knowledge by and of authority; it was nothing more than the mere certitude which was all that Vico would allow to arise from Descartes' assertion of the consciousness of existence in thinking. Since it was a knowledge of a humanity immersed in sense, it could only be expressed in the poetic, heroic language, in concrete, imaginative, symbolic fashion. We can approach it, we can even possess it as a truth beyond mere certitude, because it contained the seeds of reason, because it was a modification of our mind, because the human mind can know whatever man has created. But, for this, we must again create it in ourselves, must divest ourselves of our rational nature so far as to embody with our imagination the conditions of the men immersed in sense; yet we must retain our rational nature in order to see this knowledge in its causes and in relation to the whole life of mind in history. But since it is not knowledge of a purely rational subject-matter, we require for it not merely reason but the study of fact, of authority, of what has happened. This, too, is a condition for the possibility of a philosophy of history; for if history could be evolved from our rational nature alone, its philosophy would be identical with the philosophy of reason.

Now all these marks of a philosophy of history are to be found in Vico's work, and in the work of no thinker before him. And our admiration is raised to astonishment when we realize that Vico not only created the philosophy of history, but to a large extent the history as well. He not only explained the inner meaning of the Homeric heroes or the patriarchal monarchy, or the conflict between patricians and plebeians, but he had first to establish the actual character of these institutions, to ascertain who really ruled society in those ages, what were the motives of public order and what was the succession of political, social and linguistic forms. That he was wrong in many guesses and even in a number of generalizations was inevitable and scarcely detracts from our admiration. That we no longer attribute early religion to fear, that we have discovered magic as the ancestor of religion, that we are no longer certain about the separate origins of civilization and are going back to a belief in the individual Homer, should not blind us to the greatness of the thinker who first conceived of history as an independent, unique and necessary phase of reality, who so conceived the successive modifications of our mind in history that he was able, by applying his conception to the records of the past—to poems, chronicles and myths—to reveal the essential character of periods long misunderstood. Expressed in this way the achievement ceases to seem impossible, but it remains stupendous.

The relation between the physical world and the world of mind, between extension and thought, so elaborately set forth by Spinoza in pages which perhaps Vico did not read, is a problem treated very differently by the two philosophers. Vico sets between the two worlds a profound gulf. The physical universe was not created by man. God alone created and understands it. But in Vico's philosophy of history the two natures are combined in man. Because of his physical body man is subjected to physical needs, to passions arising from the body and to the changes in his physical environment. This affects the nature of history in two ways. Our knowledge of history is imperfect because of the admixture with the mental world of this physical coefficient of which God alone has true knowledge. In proportion as the physical coefficient is important, and it is preponderantly so in the early stages of man's development, history is a science rather of certitude than of truth, and our study of it must be more pedestrian and inductive. In the second place it prevents Vico's philosophy from being purely a philosophy of mind. The events of history, and the modifications of our mind that create institutions and the difference of times, are partly determined not so much by man's nature as by man's place in Nature. Though Vico has not ignored the influence of climate and of geographical conditions in shaping the character of peoples, he has not contributed on this element in the evolution of society and nations anything so comprehensive as was soon to be afforded by Montesquieu and a generation later and much more fully by Herder. Vico studied the physical needs of man rather under the influence of his dominant idea of separate origins of culture. The same laws of development acting on communities widely separated in time and place give the same or similar results. The same needs, the desire of the same utilities, and, finally, the same common sense of religious awe and shame and the same discovery of the superior efficacy of social co-operation over solitary self-defence operated everywhere. This part of Vico's theory is therefore rather a psychology of men as uniform individuals than a study of the varieties of human culture springing each from its appropriate soil by the rivers of Mesopotamia or between the mountain-ranges of sea-girt Hellas. In another way, however, the immersion in sense of early mankind is important in Vico's philosophy as affecting his doctrine of Providence. The history of mankind is not evolved purely from the seeds of truth in man, but from the overruling by Providence, especially in early, and in rather late and decadent periods, of actions performed for ends which, in themselves, are unrelated to man's true nature. In dragging his women into caves to escape the fear of thunder, man had no idea of founding the institution of the family or the religion of auspices or the patrician order. In exacting toilsome labour from his serfs, the "hero" had no intention of impelling them to band themselves into a community. In the ages of decline, the Epicurean or Cartesian individualists who neglected the state had no intention of causing the inclusion of that state in a wider empire and a larger unity of equal justice. But the hand of Providence is always seen by Vico as acting in accordance with law, never as the instrument of an arbitrary divine will; and it is no mere corollary but the central proposition of the new science that the creative mind which produces the world of institutions is the mind of man.

With regard to the aim and goal of the whole historic process, Vico's belief probably developed somewhat as follows. Before he came to be critical of Plato he saw in Plato's Republic, with some faults rectified by Christianity, the ideal commonwealth. His researches into the origins of language and society showed him that Plato had not understood the ways of Providence in the education of mankind. The philosophic state was the right one, certainly, in the fullness of time. But the "heroic" order was at an earlier stage the necessary and only possible one, and was likewise a theatre of virtues, an expression of ultimate values and alone the source and condition of sublime poetry. His famous doctrine of recurrence was not therefore necessarily pessimistic. It did not mean that a succession of generations worked up to an end which expressed for a brief period the beauty of reason but were themselves devoid of good, like a dark stream illuminated at distant intervals. The aim and goal is attained not only by the final generation in each historic cycle but by every generation in a different way. In the later stages came lucid thought and the sway of equal

law; in the earlier the magnanimity of those who pro-
tected the fugitives from the savages of the forest; and the
sublime imaginings of Homer and of Dante. The strenuous
nature of Vico had something in it of the spirit that
finds good in the labour to attain truth as well as in the
truth itself. Yet he complained often of the years of hard
meditation, and the signs of decay which he thought he
saw in the philosophic perversions of his time were not to
him a matter of indifference.

He experienced as fully as any great poet, for the
Scienza Nuova is a great poem, the solitary recompense
attained in creation. He had the "divine joy in this mortal
body to contemplate in the divine ideas this world of
nations in their whole extent of places, times and diver-
sities." It was the joy he promised to his readers, but
generations were to pass before they entered the land he
had seen from his height of contemplation. In his own
city his immediate successors had only glimpses of the
buried treasure of his thought; in the world beyond he
was almost unknown. One Spanish writer[79] on aesthetics
adopted his ideas of the poetic age and called the *Scienza
Nuova* a celebrated work, but the *Scienza Nuova* lay, so
far as we can tell, unread in the library of Montesquieu.[50]
The first group of thinkers to whom Vico became a living
influence were the new school of law-reformers at Naples
in the last quarter of the eighteenth century. Their leader,
Filangieri, showed the revered volume to Goethe in
March 1787. "He made me acquainted," writes Goethe,
"with an old author in whose unfathomable depths
these modern law-enthusiasts find the greatest stimulus
and edification. His name is Giambattista Vico; they
prefer him to Montesquieu. Glancing rapidly over the

pages of the book, which they presented to me as something sacred, I saw that it contained Sibylline presentiments of the good and the just that would or should hereafter come to birth, based upon serious contemplations of life and tradition. It is a beautiful thing when a people has such a patriarch. The text of Hamann will perhaps one day appear in this light to the Germans."[80] But "the first writer to study Vico's work with a true understanding of it" was Vincenzo Cuoco.[81] Cuoco says that Vico lived a hundred years before he could be appreciated, that he was the first to see that there must always have been a reason underlying legislation, a reason based on the general order of things, and that civil institutions are all subject to this order. Cuoco planned an edition of Vico, but writing in 1804 from Milan where he was a refugee, he informed his correspondent that the collections which he had made for this purpose were destroyed in the "anglo-russo-turco-napoletano" sack of Naples in 1799. Vico's son Gennaro was still living to be consulted about this proposed edition and also by Villarosa, who did actually commence the series of republications of Vico in 1818, thirteen years after Gennaro's death.[82]

Herder knew Vico's work, though he assimilated very little of his philosophy, and Jacobi recognized the affinity with Kant; but the first to reveal Vico to Europe at large was Michelet, by his *Discours* and translations, in 1827. Michelet had a profound knowledge of Vico, whom he called his only master. He sees precisely the essential difference between Vico and Herder: "In order to see man, Herder places himself in Nature, Vico in man himself, in man humanizing himself by society." He wrote of Vico rhapsodically: "Above all, an immense poetry of history, the inspiration of the tomb of Virgil, the echo of the two Tuscans who have sung of ancient Italy; Virgil and Dante; finally, in a reminiscent melancholy the Etruscan doctrine of epochs, the thought of a regular rotation of the natural and civil world in which under the eye of Providence all the peoples take up the song of the eternal choir of life and death. There is Naples and there is Vico." This is perhaps more poetical than accurate. The expressions "reminiscent melancholy" and "under the eye of Providence" contain wrong suggestions. Michelet interprets more accurately when he says: "The word uttered in the *Scienza Nuova* is this: humanity is its own work. God acts upon it but by means of it."

The intellectual atmosphere of the nineteenth century was ready for a reception of Vico. Those who lived after him had, in a sense, to prepare the way for him in the development of ideas. Both the critical philosophy and romanticism contributed. The striking resemblance between his speculations and the theories of Wolf and Niebuhr helped to attract attention to this prophetic figure in the region of historical research. The reaction from abstract theories of politics found itself to have been anticipated. Amid the rapid accumulation of historical knowledge the search for the laws of progress was undertaken with some hope of success, and in this path also Vico had gone before.

But most important of all remains Vico the philosopher. The Neapolitan Hegelians of the middle of the nineteenth century, with Spaventa at their head, found that in the criticism of Hegel, in dealing with the deficiencies and difficulties of Hegel, the ideas and suggestions of Vico came to their assistance. From these are directly descended the Italian leaders of Vichian interpretation at the present day, for whom the philosophy of Vico is no dead thing. If any proof of this is needed, it is perhaps sufficient to remark how questions about the interpretation of Vico tend to become confused or identified with the problems themselves with which Vico deals. The Catholic has his own Vico, the positivist his, and the idealist metaphysician also his own. This is not merely a result of Vico's obscurity. It is partly because of the profundity with which he examined problems yet unsolved.

Translation of

"AFFETTI DI UN DISPERATO"
1693

WEARIED I pray, my bitter torments all,
In memory's dim region be conjoined
If ever ye be courteous torturers;
For ye so many dolorous changes deal
I know ye not and yet I feel ye still,
And fear to number my calamities.
Would that the heat of sorrow's kindled breath
Under the arch of sight heavy with tears
Could dry up my lament,
And ye, my tears, driven back to my sad heart,
Drown there in vindication of yourselves
The wounding sighs. Leave not a moment free
For the heart's cruel bitter pain to die,
Or void that lodging where affections dwell;
For I desire, till I shall be no more,
To keep ye in my breast, if what feeds life
Ever can bring me to my journey's bourn.

For now the iron age draws to its fall,
The Fates for our destruction are arrayed;
Our ills like to our crimes are grown so great
Beyond the altitude of earlier times;
Under the weight of novel maladies
We groan and weaken, pallid, frail and bowed,
And our life's wings flit swifter to the tomb.
Misfortune fruitful of calamities
Not known of old and not imagined yet
And unbelievable even to those
Who undergo them most, so darkens heaven,

It seems no gentle light, no blessed spirit
Can thence descend again. Yet he who most
In such strange ways of ill is exercised,
Could he behold the face of the dire Fate
That pities not in punishment of me,
Would bless his own for being merciful.

The living soul of every breathing thing
That to the threshold of this life draws near
Accepts its bodily burden with delight,
Happily friended in its instruments.
But either cruel and disdainful chance
Or stars ungenerous or nature strayed
Composed me of two foes, a mortal part
Weary and weak and with afflictions full,
That now meseems is failing, and assails
The spirit with all foul and bitter griefs;
And a soul full of cares unpitying that
Makes of the body ruin and a plague.
And when I enter with close frequent thought
And find myself at war against myself,
No member have I answering to the soul
That has no virtue to awake the sense
Save in the effect of angry scorn and pain,
And in my dolorous course no hope of peace.

And yet in part it seems my grief is less
By the fierce joy of my continual plaint,
Therefore myself more to involve in pain
I will sustain my sorrow with its foe,
And sing in gentle harmonies of all
That is most happy; I will sing of life
More tranquil than mortality has known,
Of moderate pleasures, honourable delights,
Treasures by merit won, renown deserved,
A mind, in its celestial robe, at peace;
I'll crown my grief, unequalled that it shine,

Singing of love whose only wage is love
And mutual tender faith. And all of these
Through my fell thought regarded by my heart
Shall overbrim its grief, as ruddy gems
Held for a medium to the physical sight
Turn milk to blood, and make a flame of ice.

What favour of yours can ye reproach me with,
O cruel stars? Go track it if ye may
'Mid thwarted blessings of celestial powers.
I know at least this of myself, that never
Was respite without woe to follow it.
Wherefore, alas, was I, from the blest world,
Led, by a weary path, broken and wrecked
Down to this day of bitterest despair?
For ever when I gaze back on my time,
On days, months, years expended all in pain,
I see that I was born to destinies
Of cruelty alone, sighs, flame, tears, death.
If the fierce troubles of my ruinous days
Part me not yet into my elements,
It must be that my fate is taking pause
To make more terrible my last abyss,
Or else the very greediness of death
Fears to be bitterer by taking me.

True, from some brighter region of the sky
Came down to me the longing to awaken,
By beechen root and under laurel shades,
The beauteous radiance of illustrious souls.
To my sad spirit that in part was given
When it put on the veil that shadows it;
So that it seems to look upon itself
And ask itself what sort of self it is.
Oh! sad one, wondering how to name itself.
But such I call no gift, punishment rather;
He suffers most who understands his woe.

Oh! blest, and in your ignorance content,
Ye nymphs and shepherds, who for all your toils
Can find your peace again in rustic fare,
Apples or milk. To whom nor frost nor heat
Is other than delight, the shade of boughs,
Or homely consecration of the hearth;
Who need no other joys than your rude loves,
Or pleasant weariness of rustic chase.

But me, what joy remains for me to follow,
Weary, o'erwhelmed, abandoned and alone,
In this most wretched life I still must lead?
I am a tedious burden to the earth,
Fruitless, a stock, a stone; yet these have peace,
As in Earth's centre. My delight should be
To fade away; but Fate refuses that.
Then be it so, and, if I am reserved
Still for this sighing and lamentful life,
Let still the rain of miseries, the rain
Of bitter destiny fall on my head.
And spare me not, for I should estimate it
For poverty not pity in the Fates.
Or I should think from envy I was grudged
The miserable primacy of grief,
And to be as a beacon to the wretched.
But by my sorrows now I take this oath,
Ye grisly wastes and horrid, lone, sad woods,
Never shall, whilst I breathe, one sigh of mine
Your profound ancient silences disturb.

My song, remain alone to weep with me,
Where sorrow dwells, and go not among men
Seeking the pity that my woe contemns.
But if a grief lamented is less felt
My stricken heart will scorn that you remain,
Jealous not to divide the lone despair.

NOTES AND REFERENCES

1. For a refutation of the theory that Vico's philosophy is scholastic see Croce: *Fonti della gnoseologia vichiana*: and Gentile: *Studi vichiani* (1927), pp. 142–6. Werner, an important biographer both of Vico and of Suarez, does not trace any of Vico's doctrine to the writings of Suarez.

2. The description of Vatolla in Vico's time and many biographical details I owe to Nicolini: *La giovanezza di Giambattista Vico*.

3. *Opera* (Ferrari, 1836), VI, pp. 42, 47.

4. For a profound study of this subject see Carl Gebhardt: *Spinoza, von den Festen und Ewigen Dingen, Einleitung*.

5. Nicolini, op. cit., p. 194.

6. Gentile: *Studi Vichiani*, p. 64.

7. Quoted by Wicksteed: *Relations between Dogma and Philosophy*, p. 279 f.

8. *Discours de la Méthode*, Part IV.

9. A. Boyce Gibson: *The Philosophy of Descartes*, p. 106. "The view that the content of ideas requires an efficient cause was strange to the pre-Cartesian philosophies."

10. Vico says 1701; but see Gentile, op. cit., p. 78 n.

11. For the researches of Signor Donati on the chronology of the orations see Gentile, op. cit., pp. 98–103. For the MSS. see *Oraz. Inaug.*, pp. 305 ff. (edition of 1914).

12. *Novum Organum*, Aphorism II. Vico has *adjumenta* for Bacon's *auxilia*.

13. *Oraz. Inaug.* (1914), p. 78.

14. Capua facundo perfusus pectore vino, etc.; Cotugno, op. cit., p. 35.

15. For a full treatment of the question of originality see Croce: *Le fonti della gnoseologia vichiana*, also *Filosofia di G. B. Vico*, p. 4.

16. *Kritik der Reinen Vernunft, Vorrede zur zweiten Auflage*.

17. *Opera* (Ferrari, 1835), Vol. III, p. 23.

18. Flint: *Vico, a Critical Biography*, p. 125.

19. Crescimbene: *La vita degli Arcadi illustri*, quoted by Donati: *Autografi e documenti*, p. 89.

20. Life by Giannantonio Sergio, prefixed to Gravina's Italian works (1757).

21. It is largely through his discovery of the correspondence of Avitabile that Signor Donati has been able to give the full history of the Neapolitan Arcadians for 1710 in *Autografi e Documenti*, pp. 67–142.

22. Lib. I, cap. I.

23. *Opera* (Ferrari, 1835), II, p. 329.

24. De nostri temporis studiorum ratione, in *Oraz. Inaug.*, p. 95 (edition of 1914).

25. Op. cit., p. 189.

26. *De Ortu*, p. 1 (edition of 1717).

27. See quotation in Cotugno: *La Sorte di G. B. Vico*, pp. 192–3.

28. J. G. Robertson: *The Genesis of Romantic Theory*, esp. pp. 192 ff.; and Cotugno, op. cit., pp. 159 ff. and 192 ff.

29. The paragraphs in the *De Uno* giving the above scheme are X, LXXI–LXXV, LXXXVI–XCIX, CI, CVIII–CXVIII. *Opera* (Ferrari), Vol. III.

30. *De Uno*, XLIV, LX, LXIII.

31. § CIV.

32. §§ CIV, CXXIX, CXXXI, and footnote to CXCII.

33. §§ CXLI–CXLV.

34. § CCXVIII.

35. See a very thorough study of these theories and controversies in relation to Vico in A. Sorrentino: *La Retorica e la Poetica di G. B. Vico*.

36. P. Arcari: *Processi e Rappresentazioni di Scienza Nuova*, pp. 53 ff.

37. *Opera* (Ferrari), Vol. III. *De Const. Philol.*, cap. XII, § XIX.

38. *De Const. Philol.*, nota in Exornationem Perpetuam, cap. XII.

39. Cap. XXIV.

40. Nota, ad ornatum capitis XXIII.

41. Chapters XIII, XX, XXIII, XXIV, XXX.

42. B. Brugi: *Rileggendo l'autobiografia di G. B. Vico: in Rivista internazionale di filosofia del diritto* (1925), (*Per il secondo centenario della Scienza Nuova*), pp. 12–19. Also Croce: *La Critica* (1908), VI, pp. 308–10.

43. For the whole history of the different editions of the *Scienza Nuova* see Nicolini: *Introduzione dell' Editore* (to the great edition of 1911).

44. Croce: *Bibliografia vichiana* (1904), p. 95; also in *Autobiografia*, etc. (1911), p. 167; and the last-named volume for all quotations from Vico's correspondence.

45. *De Uno*, LXVIII; *Scienza Nuova* (1725), II, 2, and the edition of 1911, I, Sec. 2, cap. 12.

46. For Vico's tendency to pantheism see Croce: *La filosofia di G. B. Vico*, cap. XII.

47. Op. cit., pp. 40 ff.

48. Cf. Hegel: *Die Vernunft in der Geschichte*, II, i, (*d*):— Die Individuen treten in sich zurück und streben nach eigenen Zwecken.

49. J. G. Robertson: op. cit.

50. Croce: *La filosofia di G. B. Vico*, p. 317; a phrase here and there seems to show that Montesquieu at least opened the *Scienza Nuova*:—il (sc. Dieu) agit selon ces règles, parce qu'il les connaît; il les connaît parce qu'il les a faites. (Esprit des Lois, cap. 1.)

51. Arcari, op. cit., p. 21.

52. January 12, 1729.

53. The letter to Porcia of September 16, 1725, proves that it was in Porcia's hands by that date.

54. Croce: *La filosofia di G. B. Vico*, p. 311.

55. A hostile criticism was made by Giannone in a private letter (Croce in *La Critica* (1917), p. 195, gives the quotation).

56. Nicolini: *Per la biografia di G. B. Vico*. Gentile: *Studi Vichiani*. B. Donati: *Autografi e Documenti*.

57. *Prefazione dell' Editore* (to the edition of 1836), pp. x ff. For Croce's reply see *La filosofia di G. B. Vico*, p. 311.

58. See *Opera* (Ferrari, 1836), IV, p. 345, for the text of the review. Vico's letter to Giacchi is December 4, 1729. Giannone has been suspected, but, as Croce points out, could not have been the culprit, since he was not in Naples.

59. *Joh. Baptistae Vici* in *Acta Eruditorum Lipsiensia Notae*, often referred to as Vici Vindiciae, 1729.

60. Croce: *Saggio sullo Hegel*, etc., Part II, pp. 287 ff., for a comparison with other theories of the ludicrous.

61. This account is based on the *Frammento di Prefazione all' Edizione del* 1744, but is not easy to reconcile with Vico's additions to the autobiography, where the story is, however, less clear. See Nicolini's edition of the *Scienza Nuova* (1911), Vol. I, XXXIII.

62. For a complete study of the causes of Vico's obscurity see Nicolini, in his preface to the edition of 1911. See also Arcari, op. cit., pp. 20 ff.

63. Edition of 1911, p. 188.

64. Pp. 258–60.

65. P. 301.

66. P. 605.

67. Finzler: *Homer in der Neuzeit*. Finzler thinks Vico knew nothing of d'Aubignac. Croce: *La filosofia di G. B. Vico*, cap. XVI. *Cambridge Ancient History*, Vol. II, p. 502. "In this essay (of d'Aubignac) we have the germs of the Homeric heresies of the nineteenth century" (J. B. Bury).

68. J. G. Robertson, op. cit., pp. 24 ff. and 60 ff.

69. *Scienza Nuova* (1911), p. 767.

70. "Centro di una vera e propria scuola letteraria, non ancora ben nota e degna di essere studiata" (Gentile: *Studi Vichiani*, p. 206).

71. Villarosa's *Aggiunta* to the Autobiography. For Spinelli, his education by Caloprese and his controversy with Doria see his own autobiography in *Raccolta d'Opuscoli scientifici e filologici*, tom. 49 (Venice, 1753).

72. The letter is given in Gentile, op. cit., pp. 221–2.

73. Croce: *Autobiografia, etc., di G. B. Vico*, pp. 223–4.

74. Gentile, op. cit., pp. 210 ff., 221 ff. and 226–8.

75. Both Ferrari and Nicolini publish the edition of 1744 showing the differences of that of 1730. Nicolini, however, quite supersedes Ferrari, not only by correcting the text but by showing all the changes (in the *Correzioni, miglioramenti e aggiunti*) between 1730 and 1744.

76. J. G. Robertson, *Genesis of Romantic Theory*, p. 193. Professor Robertson, who thinks both Gravina and Muratori were impressed by Mazzoni's *Difesa di Dante*, considered that Signor Croce underrates Gravina's influence on Vico. For Mazzoni see above, pp. 38–9.

77. Discourse for the Academy of Nicolo Salerni (1736) in *Opera* (Ferrari), vol. VI, p. 55.

78. First *Scienza Nuova*, I, 6.

79. *Ignacio de Luzan*. See J. G. Robertson, op. cit., p. 220.

80. Italienische Reise, March 5, 1787.

81. Croce: *La filosofia di Giambattista Vico*, p. 135.

82. Gentile, op. cit., p. 295.

INDEX